The forgotten philanthropist

The story of George Herbert Lawrence

This fascinating story is of an unassuming individual with a strong urge to do whatever he possibly could for those he considered less fortunate than himself.

Here was a self-made man who was determined to distribute quite large amounts of money earned through his successful Sheffield razor blade manufacturing business, before being killed in the first blitz on Sheffield in 1940.

It tells how he helped his adopted Derbyshire village of Hathersage to obtain facilities they could never have dreamed of owning, at the time of the Great Depression and how, through his friendship with a former Lord Mayor of Sheffield, William Farewell Wardley, he also assisted that city, and certain towns in France and Belgium in the aftermath of the Great War.

It tells of how enduring his legacy has been, and how his benefactions still serve their communities today.

Front cover Caricature of George Herbert Lawrence as depicted in the Sheffield Telegraph.

Left Decorated border from an illuminated book presented to George Lawrence in recognition of his gift to Sheffield of the Longley Park Pool. Decorative initials shown inside the front cover are also from the same book.

CONTENTS

IT WAS DURING 1932 that George Herbert Lawrence went to live in Hathersage, a Peak District village ten miles from Sheffield city centre. He then proceeded to donate money for several facilities there, all for the benefit of its inhabitants.

In Hathersage today, while there is the 'Lawrence Hall' there is little else that tells of his many other gifts.

After suggesting that his enduring legacy to the village was not sufficiently recognised or known about, I was encouraged to correct this omission by making residents much more aware of what he had given.

My research into his benevolence started in Hathersage, but as is the way with research, I 'followed my nose' and one thing led to another. I soon became aware that his generosity also stretched to Sheffield, to Bakewell, and even to towns in northern Europe.

I remembered seeing an article in the Sheffield Telegraph of 2nd November 2001 when Councillor (Cllr) Jackie Field (as she was then known) had visited the French First World War battlefields and had discovered a link between Bapaume there and Sheffield.

In this small town of Bapaume in Northern France George Lawrence is certainly remembered and even revered, yet to all intents and purposes he is forgotten or ignored in Sheffield. He became the forgotten philanthropist.

He donated considerable amounts of both his money and his time and nearly all this seemed to happen within the very short timescale from around 1934 until his tragic death in 1940.

It is a fact that he is not commemorated by name in many places, because of his oft-expressed wish to remain anonymous.

Armed with all this information I was able to set about my task of raising people's awareness of George Lawrence and what he had done for the benefit of so many people, first by a series of illustrated talks and then by this publication.

The book has been made possible only with the tremendous help of Bernard Madden who has designed it and spent hours 'moulding' it into shape, and Richard Kemp, my proof-reader, whose dexterity has made it far more readable. Thanks also to Katy Burgin, George Lawrence's great-niece, for the loan of her family memorabilia. Photographs have come from various sources most of which are acknowledged later, but Simon Bull has taken and produced several 'to order', shots which deserve particular mention.

My special thanks must be accorded to Hathersage Gala Committee and Hathersage Parish Council for their financial support, thus enabling any profit from this book to be donated to King George's Field fund for the benefit of Hathersage Swimming pool and surrounding facilities.

For the sake of brevity I have often used GHL or George Lawrence when referring to him in the text.

I have also tried to make more meaningful the 1930's, 1940's and 1950's money quoted. I have added in parentheses what the equivalent money value would be in today's terms, although this does not always give a true reflection on the difference. For instance, the Retail Price Index (RPI) is now roughly about 50 times what it was in 1930, yet average earnings are now nearly 200 times higher. This difference illustrates how, for most people, the buying power of each pound and so their standard of living has increased.

Someone doing a similar job now can buy far more things than 80 years ago. For instance, one probably has a motorcar, and a house, and one goes away on foreign holidays. Un-thought of then.

Improvements in mechanisation and automation have helped to keep manufactured cost increases down below RPI, but building costs have increased well above that index largely due to the high labour proportion involved and also to massive increases in land costs. In these cases a modern estimate of costs has sometimes been shown as well.

So while such estimates as have been made are not definitive, I am sure they will help the reader to understand the enormity of the Lawrences' generosity.

Brian Ward *Hathersage July 2011*

👉 Who was he?

FROM HUMBLE BEGINNINGS GEORGE HERBERT LAWRENCE became a 'philanthropist extraordinaire'.

George Lawrence was originally from Italian stock. His great grandfather, Sebastian Lorenzo, was born in Leghorn, Italy in about 1799 and came to Sheffield where he married Harriet Youle, a local girl, in Rotherham in April 1829, by which time he had anglicised his surname to Lawrence.

Sebastian was a glass silverer by trade, one who applied the silver backing to mirrors, although by the time of his death in 1869 he was described as a silver engraver.

They lived in Tudor Street, poor working class accommodation near the centre of Sheffield but there is no trace of the family in the 1841 census. This could be for a variety of reasons, possibly they returned to Italy, although they were certainly in this country by 1844 when George's grandfather, James, was born in Sheffield.

On 3rd June 1888 James's son, John Francis (George's father), married Martha Jane Thompson, at St Philip's Church, Infirmary Road, Sheffield (since demolished).

On their wedding certificate both were shown as living in Infirmary Road, and at that time Martha's father and John's father were both listed as grinders - presumably of cutlery.

George Herbert Lawrence was born on 5th Oct 1888 (four months after his parents' wedding), where his birth certificate shows him at Court 12, Fitzwilliam Street, his father John then being shown as a journeyman engraver. Ten years later, by 1898 he was living on Eyre Street and was attending St Paul's Church school. This would have been St Paul's Parish Church where the Peace Gardens are now found.

St Philip's Church
(now demolished)

By the 1901 census his father had separated from his mother and George (aged 13) and his two sisters, Beatrice Esther and Mary Jane, were living with James Fretwell at 63 Eyre Street, with his father John and James Fretwell's daughter Ada Fretwell, apparently a cousin of George. His father John was then also a silver engraver.

As can be seen, George Lawrence was from very working class stock.

As he grew up he became a seller of the 'Star' evening newspaper, running miles each night to earn a few pence, and then started work as a barber's 'lather boy', earning two shillings a week.

He later became apprenticed into razor grinding and it was said that this is when he saw the possibilities of mass razor production.

In 1913 at the age of 25, he started his own business in a tiny shed in Porter Lane, Sheffield, which he rented at 5/- a week, employing three or four men and turning out safety razor blades with "crude and unsatisfactory tools".

When he started, there were perhaps only two others in Sheffield, John Watts and R S Mitchell, making what was known in the trade as 'wafer' safety blades, for at that time most blades of this type came from Germany.

Surrey Street Methodist Church
(now demolished)

His marriage took place on 27th December 1916 when he was age 28, in the Surrey Street United Methodist Church. His wife, Elsie Bolton, being 27 was described as a "Razor Warehouse Woman", of 1 Neill Road, off Ecclesall Road, Sheffield (near the Hunters Bar roundabout), while George was shown as still living at 63 Eyre Street. Her father James Bolton, by then deceased, had been a table-knife cutler. George and Elsie were never to have children.

When the war broke out, at 25 years of age, GHL should have been eligible for military service but he did not serve in the armed forces. Maybe his was a 'protected' occupation, for many of the earliest servicemen who volunteered soon after the outbreak of war, were later released to return to their civilian jobs. Their absence had been found to be causing severe disruption to essential wartime production.

A history of shaving

IT CAN BE SAID that since the first man arrived on the earth, a decision has had to be made - whether to allow a beard to grow or to remove it. Cave paintings have shown that, contrary to popular opinion, early man went about his work clean-shaven, making good use of pieces of sharpened flint. With the Bronze Age and primitive metalworking came razors made from iron, bronze and even gold. The civilisations of Rome and Greece used iron blades with long handles and developed the shape of the 'open' or 'cut-throat' razor, which was the only practical razor until the 19th century. With improvements in steel manufacture came blades that were really sharp and capable of being re-sharpened.

Advances in razor technology changed shaving habits in the 20th century. In 1900, most men were either shaved by the local barber (your trusted confidant, wielding a cut-throat razor), or periodically at home, when required rather than regularly. The barber's better-off customers would have a personal set of seven razors, labelled 'Sunday' to 'Saturday'. Today, most men shave every day in their own homes, using a wide variety of equipment.

A Frenchman, Jean-Jacques Perret, who was inspired by the joiner's plane, invented the first 'safety' razor, where the skin is protected from all but the very edge of the blade. An expert on the subject, he also wrote a book called *Pogonotomy or the Art of Learning to Shave Oneself.*

In the late 1820s, a similar razor was made in Sheffield and from the 1870s, a single-edge blade, mounted on a hoe-shaped handle was available in Britain and Germany.

The idea of a use-once, disposable blade, which didn't need re-sharpening, came from King Camp Gillette, an American, in 1895. It was suggested to him that the ideal way to make money was to sell a product, part of which would need replacing at frequent intervals. An early example of built-in obsolescence. However, producing a wafer-thin piece of steel with a sharpened edge strong enough to remove a beard was a near technical impossibility at that time. Although patents were filed in 1901, it was not until 1903 that Gillette could go into business with the assistance of his technical adviser, William Nickerson, who gave the necessary financial backing. He produced a grand total of 51 razors and 168 blades in that year. To generate interest, many razors were given away to his friends.

By 1905, the year the Gillette razor came to Britain, 90,000 razors and 2.5 million blades were produced, rising to 0.3 million razors and 14 million blades in 1908.

During World War I, the U.S. Government issued Gillette safety razors to their entire armed forces. By the end of the war, some 3.5 million razors and 32 million blades had been put into military hands, thereby converting an entire nation to the Gillette safety razor.

Blades for the European market were then being made in Germany under licence from Gillette, but in 1914 when the First World War started, the German-made blades were no longer admitted into this country. GHL obviously took full advantage of this situation: three years after starting his works he married and had £400 in the bank (£20,000 today).

In 1920, the Gillette razor was introduced as standard issue to the British Army, replacing the old 'cut-throat' razors.

The early standard Gillette pattern of safety 'Wafer' blades, were 6 thousandths of an inch in thickness [*0.006inches or 0.15mm], and were originally sharpened by hand. The grinding wheel was fixed and the blade was put on a moveable table and it was traversed under the wheel by lever action. The blade was then turned over, then turned round and over again, to sharpen all the four sides.

Gillette's early models had a separate handle and clamp unit for the blade, but in the 1930s they introduced a single-piece version which had opening 'wings' in the top for inserting the blade. Other razor manufacturers, such as Wilkinson, Ever-Ready and Valet, had produced similar safety razors, but with blades that could be resharpened. These used a new version of the old leather strop, or a stropping machine, through which the blade was passed. Tiny safety razors for women, using the Gillette system, appeared in the 1920s.

Later the increasing popularity of the rival electric razor prompted further technical development in the late 1950s and 1960s onwards: long-life stainless steel blades were introduced by Wilkinson Sword in 1956 and twin-blade safety razors came in the 1960s, along with the completely disposable, one-piece plastic razor introduced by Bic.

A Frenchman, Jean-Jacques Perret, who was inspired by the joiner's plane, invented the first 'safety' razor, where the skin is protected from all but the very edge of the blade. An expert on the subject, he also wrote a book called *Pogonotomy or the Art of Learning to Shave Oneself.*

👉 His Works

83 and 85 Southgrove Road today

WHITE SHEFFIELD TRADE DIRECTORY 1919/20, shows only G H Lawrence and H Innocent & Son as 'Razor Blade manufacturers' and that GHL and his wife were living at 85 Southgrove Road (off Ecclesall Road, almost opposite the Berkeley Precinct). This was also his business address. Then, a little later, his home address changed to number 83 - next door, while his business remained at no 85.

In the 1925 Kelly Trade Directory, George H Lawrence Works were at 32 Eyre Street and his home at 85 Southgrove Road.

In 1926 he joined the Sheffield Chamber of Commerce and by 1929 he was still trading at Eyre Street, as owner of the "famous Laurel Safety Razor Blade Company", before moving his works in December 1930 to 13 Brunswick Road, Burngreave.

In November 1930 the firm became registered as a 'limited liability' company with GHL as managing director. He had by then adopted the slogan "Laurel blades for Hardy beards", an obvious play on the famous screen stars Laurel & Hardy.

Brunswick Road was not far from 78 Nursery Street, which became his works in 1932. This building had previously been the Sheffield Children's Hospital. Sheffield Children's Hospital (East End) started off at 86 The Wicker in 1893, before moving in 1913 to this purpose-built building on Nursery Street, and which was also an Isolation Hospital for contagious diseases. A lady once came into the works and said she had been treated there as a child.

Left top Southgrove Road
Left below Nursery Street
Laurel Works 1933

'Laurel blades for Hardy beards' became the adopted sales line for the GHL business.

👉 1932

THE HOSPITAL MOVED AGAIN in 1931, which enabled George Lawrence to acquire the property in January 1932, the works in Brunswick Road having proved totally inadequate.

Laurel and Hardy the famous film stars, visited Sheffield on 4th August 1932 where they made personal appearances on stage at the Cinema House. Their films "Helpmates", "Our Dogs" and "Trader Hound" were being shown at the time. They stayed at the Grand Hotel next door. Stan Laurel's mother Mrs Jefferson and Oliver Hardy's wife were in the group.

Stan Laurel was reported as saying he had not visited Sheffield since 1909 when he appeared at the Empire with Fred Karno and Charlie Chaplin in "Jimmy the Fearless". Shortly afterwards he went to America for the first time, with Fred Karno's comedies.

It has been suggested that, at GHL's invitation, Laurel and Hardy actually stayed at 'Belmont' in Hathersage. This is unlikely as they were reported as making stage appearances at 6.50 pm and 9.00 pm the day they arrived in Sheffield from Leeds, and were leaving the next morning for Birmingham.

However it can be assumed George Lawrence did meet them, for he certainly reproduced an advertisement in which he used his slogan "Laurel Blades for Hardy Beards", alongside the newspaper coverage that day in both the Sheffield Star and Sheffield Telegraph, and he must have had their agreement to use their names. In fact he later received a letter from Stan Laurel dated 31st December 1932 from 'Kal E Reach Studio', Culver City, California. This suggests he had also presented Stan with a 'Laurel' razor during his visit.

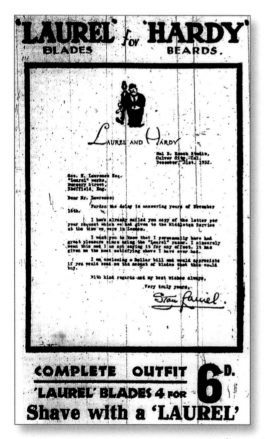

Dear Mr Lawrence,

Pardon the delay in answering yours of November 16th.

I have already mailed you copy of the letter per your request which we had given to Middleton Service at the time we were in London.

I want you to know that I personally have had great pleasure since using the 'Laurel' razor. I sincerely mean this and I am not saying it for any effect. It has given me the most satisfying shave I have ever had.

I am enclosing a Dollar bill and would appreciate if you would send me the amount of blades that this would buy.

With kind regards and my best wishes always,

Very truly yours,

Stan Laurel.

An interesting fact about Stan Laurel, born in Ulverston in the Lake District on 16th June 1890 as Arthur Stanley Jefferson, is that he was married six times to only five different women, and was divorced four times.

'Belmont', the Lawrence home
in Hathersage

It was about the same time, in 1932 that George Lawrence moved from Sheffield to live in the nearby village of Hathersage. He bought 'Belmont' on Jaggers Lane from John Arthur Stead, another Sheffield razor blade manufacturer, whom he knew. Mr Stead had moved his home to 'Barnfield House' in the same village and was a leading light in Hathersage Methodist Church there.

☛ **1933**

WHEN GHL EXHIBITED for the first time at the British Industries Fair in 1933, he called in Stanley Dickson Technical Advertising Service to design a most attractive stand. Stanley Dickson's son, Roger Dickson, later took over the company's helm, which eventually became S.D.D. Exhibitions Ltd. They still operate, now from their new offices in Parkway Business Park, Sheffield.

GHL had set about extending part of the Nursery Street works and a newspaper article in May 1933 was headlined "Double the Floor Space" and "Output of 2 million weekly".

The report went on to say: "The extension by means of a fine new block to the rear, completes the island site of Nursery Street, Johnson Street, Nursery Lane and Johnson Lane. The old building at the front was the old Children's Hospital. The operating theatre is where the final stropping machines are because it gives a good light. The flat roof of the new building could be used for roller-skating; below this on the second floor is the canteen".

The plant was equipped with the most modern machines, both automatic and semi automatic, including final ones to automatically wrap the blades in their little packets.

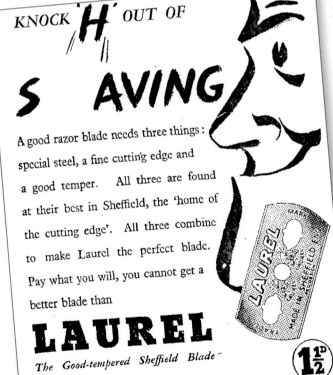

KNOCK 'H' OUT OF

S AVING

A good razor blade needs three things: special steel, a fine cutting edge and a good temper. All three are found at their best in Sheffield, the 'home of the cutting edge'. All three combine to make Laurel the perfect blade. Pay what you will, you cannot get a better blade than

LAUREL

The Good-tempered Sheffield Blade

Made by George Lawrence Ltd. of Sheffield

1½d

Including purchase tax

This is the time we first begin to see the benefits that his larger and obviously more profitable business produced, but it is very important to realize the background against which this was happening.

The country was in, or slowly recovering from, the Great Depression of the 1930's and unemployment remained high until the approach of the Second World War. Unemployment had risen in the country from 1 million to 2.5 million by the end of 1930 and Sheffield's steel and heavy industry were particularly heavily hit, and the city had almost 60,000 out of work for several years. Fortunately Lawrence's company was able to buck this trend.

The village of Hathersage would have been similarly affected. The traditional work in local light engineering works (needles and hackle-pins) had long disappeared and when the work on the Dore to Chinley railway line was opened in 1893 this source of employment was also lost to local labour. Employment in the local quarries, first producing millstones and, latterly, stonework for the nearby Derwent and Howden Reservoirs had come and gone. Work too on the Derwent Water Board's underground aqueduct had also been finished. The railway, however, provided the easy means to travel to jobs in nearby Sheffield, but as we see, these jobs now ceased to be available. George's character suggests that a lot of what the he did for the community was intentionally aimed to alleviate this situation for many hard-pressed people.

Neither did he forget his roots and his good fortune. He would employ less fortunate friends and relations and he was always caring for his workforce.

Reference is made to the staff holidays, jaunts and dinners that had been a regular feature since his earliest days in business. He once gave a dinner for his workforce at the Grand Hotel, while trips to the seaside, to the pantomime, and to football matches were regular events for them. Ever the businessman, he always included business guests, including the Sheffield Telegraph organisation on many of these occasions.

GHL was a keen amateur sportsman and angler and seemed to carry this enthusiasm over, encouraging and providing for others so they could improve themselves through these channels.

He was a junior footballer and later a league linesman and a football referee with the Sheffield & Hallamshire County Football Association. He also assisted many times with grants to needy leagues and clubs in Sheffield minor football.

GHL was elected a member of the Sheffield & Hallamshire County Football Association Council, serving from 1933-36.

George Lawrence the football referee

"Be a sport, but let the sport be clean." George Lawrence 5th July 1938

1934

FROM 1934 TO 1940 GHL was a director of Sheffield United Football Club, at Bramall Lane where he paid for improvements to the bowling green.

Probably his first act of benevolence in Hathersage was in October 1934 when he paid for electric lighting to be installed in the village school. It was recorded in the School Log Book on 31st October that "Mr G H Lawrence of Belmont, Hathersage, having personally offered to pay the cost of installing electric light in the school, the matter was referred to Rev J H Brooksbank and the electricians commenced work in the school today". Mr Jasper E Strover was the headmaster at the time.

Since 1911, lighting there had been by gas. Prior to that it was candles and lanterns and, quite often in winter, the school had to be closed early, as the pupils could not see to read, write or complete their lessons.

All this took place when the parish of Outseats (part of the same village of Hathersage), formed its own Parish Council for the first time on 5th October 1934. (Its population of 355 having exceeded the 300 then required). Outseats parish still has the reputation of being one of the largest (in area) in the country, that has no church, public house or shop. GHL became one of its first councillors, along with W Oakes of 'Five Oaks' who became chairman, and J W Froggatt who followed him into the chair in 1936. In December 1937 GHL himself took over the chair.

This was an early example of GHL's other means of 'giving', namely of his valuable time for the benefit of the community.

Mr E Hughes, another councillor elected in 1934, said the new Council would immediately deal with the Hathersage Tip, which he described as "one of the worst bits of sanitation in England". The stench and vermin on the rubbish tip constituted a serious menace to health. (This would have been the tip on Castleton Road, opposite the last house after the railway bridge).

He employed several local people at his 'Belmont' home including Elijah Littlewood as his gardener, who had previously worked there for the Stead family.

Dick Makinson who lived at Ranmoor Hill, was a chauffeur to GHL (he later drove coaches for Sheffield United Tours). Sidney Down was also a chauffeur and handyman, and Ron White (latterly of The Plough Inn) was his chauffeur at one time.

GHL had a bowling green at his house on Jaggers Lane, which remains there, although it is no longer used as such.

He also became a member of Hathersage Bowling club, which used a small green behind the George Hotel, and he became a close friend of William (Billy) Goulder who was its President and also Chairman of Hathersage Parish Council.

George's bowling green at 'Belmont', Hathersage

It was on 21st August 1934 whilst at a gala party at GHL's 'Belmont' home, that Billy Goulder, aged 55 years, had a fatal heart attack as he joined in the dancing and played bowls that evening. This sad event spurred on GHL to construct a new bowling green for the village and to dedicate it to the memory of his friend. His idea was to construct it on part of the recently acquired village children's playing field that now belonged to the Parish Council.

At the Hathersage Parish Council meeting in October 1934, the generous offer by Mr Lawrence to lay out a new bowling green was considered and accepted. It was recorded that the "most grateful thanks on behalf of the Parishioners of Hathersage and Outseats be forwarded to Mr Lawrence...". Shortly afterwards the Bowling Club was given notice to quit the George Hotel green and Mr J A Stead purchased a field from Major Shuttleworth, and he also offered to provide a green, just for the club. In the event it was decided they would use the 'Lawrence' green.

1935

The bill to Mr Lawrence for the construction of the Bowling Green and surrounding areas was said to be nearly £2,000 (£100,000 today) and it kept over 50 local men busy for nearly nine months. This averages out to £40 per man, or about 20 shillings a week, including the cost of materials used. In today's wage terms this would be more like £400 a week, and today's cost to complete the same project would probably be in the order of £150,000.

One has to remember however that GHL rarely divulged exactly how much many of his projects actually cost. The figures quoted invariably came from press reports at the time.

In its construction Major Shuttleworth gave free quarrying from his local quarry (probably High Lees quarry), to provide stone for the crazy paving around the 'Pleasance' (a pleasure ground). George Percival & Son built the walls and steps from stone supplied by J Beresford & Sons. John Thompson & Sons were the local joiners who built the pavilion and rustic fence. The turf for the green was

The new Hathersage bowling green pavilion takes shape. *L to R:* George Lawrence, W G Langley, Elsie Lawrence, Jack Froggatt, John Thompson and W Bocking

supplied by Brooke Bray & Sons, Seed Merchant of Handsworth, and laid by Fishers of Dore. Eric Sharman remembers they were getting behind, and as a local boy, being about 14 years old at the time, he helped his father to finish off the work. Brooke Bray and Sons was the same company that had laid out and constructed the garden at 'Belmont'.

Memorial plaque to 'Billy' Goulder

In spite of deluges and bad weather, R W Proctor & Sons of Chesterfield planted about 800 roses, 200 other shrubs and thousands of bedding plants around the Rest Garden.

J W Froggatt provided haulage for materials and supplied Black Rockery Stone. Thos Jackson, Joiner of Crossland Road also assisted, and Olivet Engineering Co Ltd supplied the lawn mower.

Hathersage Parish Council decided that some suitable recognition of the donor's beneficence be included in the arrangements to be made for the opening of the Bowling Green, and it was resolved "that Mr Rampley see Mr H Beresford (J Berrisford & Sons) with regard to a design required for a Dial Stone to be erected on a position at the head of the stone steps". The plaque to commemorate the occasion was fixed to the rear of this sundial pedestal facing, and in front of the Bowling Club pavilion and reads:

THIS PLEASANCE AND BOWLING GREEN WERE MADE AND PRESENTED BY
G H LAWRENCE Esq, 'BELMONT' HATHERSAGE,
TO THE PARISHIONERS OF HATHERSAGE AND OUTSEATS.
OPENED 1st JUNE, 1935, AND DEDICATED TO THE MEMORY OF
W V GOULDER Esq,
CHAIRMAN OF HATHERSAGE PARISH COUNCIL AND A HIGHLY ESTEEMED RESIDENT

Around a thousand people were said to be present at the opening, when it was given to Hathersage Parish Council 'for all time'.

At the opening ceremony, W G Langley started proceedings by thanking Mr Lawrence for his generosity. In reply GHL hastened to assure the children that damage caused to their adjacent playing field would be rectified as soon as the weather permitted. He also thanked the men who had carried out work under Mr Marsden, before the crowd broke into singing "For He's a Jolly Good Fellow". For his assistance Mrs Lawrence then presented Mr Langley with a set of woods.

The green was declared open by Brigadier General E C W D Whithall, Chairman of the Rural Playing Fields Association for Derbyshire. Mr J A Stead then asked William Goulder's widow, Mrs Clara Goulder, to unveil the plaque, and her young son Desmond presented a bouquet to Mrs Lawrence.

Bill Goulder had died less than ten months earlier yet everything was completed at the opening with the exception of final touches to the pavilion.

Hathersage Band played and GHL and other dignitaries bowled the first woods, before Hathersage Bowling Club, captained by J T Thompson, took on, and beat, invited players from Chatsworth, Calver, Bamford and Grindleford.

In August that year, the Ladies Bowling team welcomed a team from Abbeydale Park, on the same day that a wreath was laid on the memorial pillar to mark the first anniversary of William Goulder's death.

Then in December 1935, M J Gleeson Ltd, a well-known Sheffield Building Contractor, was persuaded to sell to GHL some land in Hathersage that they had recently bought, and on which they intended to build houses. Gleeson agreed they would sell if alternative land could be offered to them for their house building. It had been suggested that the rent for the proposed Gleeson's houses was going to be 15/- a week. They were obviously intended for the better off, as this was rather a lot when you see what local men earned on the Bowling Green project. Average wages were quoted as being around 28/- a week at that time - if you were in employment.

No evidence exists that any such replacement land was ever forthcoming. The deal was more probably made after persuasion by George, who wanted the land so that he could build his ambitious dream of a swimming pool, children's paddling pool, sandpit, bandstand and tennis courts, for the local community.

He felt that Hathersage possessed a very good brass band and he included a bandstand so that villagers could hear them more during the summer.

George wanted the land so that he could build his ambitious dream of a swimming pool, children's paddling pool, sandpit, bandstand and tennis courts, for the local community.

The opening ceremony at Hathersage Bowling Green - *left* Mrs Goulder unveils the memorial plaque, *right* Elsie Lawrence presents a set of woods to Mr Langley

GHL'S ORIGINAL PROPOSAL was for the Parish Council to buy the land from Gleeson's for £360, after which he would then pay for all the construction work involved. However a public meeting threw this suggestion out as it could have meant an extra 1d in the £ on the rates. It was reported: "the meeting ended in uproar".

Undeterred, he then decided to buy also the land and build everything entirely at his own expense, including various pieces of playing equipment for the adjacent children's playing field. This was put to a further meeting on 20th April 1936 when it was gratefully accepted.

Mr John Arthur Stead referred to the offer as the most magnanimous that had ever been made to Hathersage during the 35 years he had lived in the village.

The swimming pool was to be fed from the water of five nearby springs, while the children's paddling pool was to be fed from mains water.

En-Tout-Cas Company from Syston, Leicester (a well known sports facility construction company) was appointed as the main contractor for the swimming pool, tennis courts and the children's paddling pool.

C L Marcroft Ltd of Dore, constructed the children's sandpit, and the refreshment rooms and tennis changing rooms underneath the solarium. George Percival & Son of Hathersage again built the boundary wall and steps; J H Jepson of Hathersage carried out the plumbing. J W Froggatt & Son, also from the village, did the bulk of the haulage, while local J Beresford and Sons supplied dressed stone from the local Falcliffe Quarry and Leadmill Works. Charles Ross Ltd. from Heeley, Sheffield, carried out the constructional steelwork for the tearooms and solarium, and R Smith & Co of Bakewell supplied timber for seating and rustic fencing.

Following the acceptance by the Parish Council on 20th April, the construction contract was placed on 7th May and work started just 10 days later.

Just ten weeks later, and in spite of wet weather hampering the work, the pool was officially opened on 27th July 1936, after only a little over two months of construction work!

This programme was amazing when one considers the amount of work involved. There was considerable difference in levels between the pool area and the surrounding land. Strong retaining walls had to be built, the pool cast in concrete and then backfilled all the way round.

The bandstand base was constructed and the bandstand delivered and erected. The tearooms and tennis changing rooms were built with solarium over, which included 'Vita' glass panels allowing UV light from the sun to pass through. The pool changing-rooms and the ticket offices and filtration plant were built. Three diving boards were erected, all the water piping, drains and pumps were installed. The whole thing was painted and then filled with water by Sheffield Fire Brigade, and then tested, and grass surrounds and paths were laid.

Apart from manual labour they only had the mechanical assistance of a mechanical digger

John A Stead referred to the offer as the most magnanimous that had ever been made to Hathersage

17

Above Sheffield Fire Brigade filling the new swimming pool
Below Sir Charles Clegg (seated) declared the pool open

working with Turner's horse and cart, to carry out all this work. Only the Solarium was not completely finished on the opening day, a fact referred to in Sir Charles Clegg's opening speech.

In his opening address GHL's colleague at Sheffield United, Sir Charles Clegg, President of the Football Association, President of both Sheffield United and Sheffield Wednesday football clubs, who had played for England and refereed the FA Cup Final in 1882, and an ardent Methodist, said he had accepted the honour out of regard for Mr Lawrence's endeavour to promote clean, healthy sport for young and old.

He added "I have had opportunities to talk to the late King and I am sure what we are doing today would have had his full support". He was referring of course to the fact that the pool and surrounding playing fields and bowling green had become officially the **KING GEORGE'S FIELD**, one of the first in Derbyshire. This effectively protects them from future disposal and this remains the official name of the entire complex to this day.

"Sir Charles Clegg, Mr and Mrs Lawrence, Ladies and Gentlemen.

As Captain of the Church of England school I have the honour of proposing a vote of thanks to Mr and Mrs Lawrence for their generous gift to the children of Hathersage.

The Sandpit and Paddling Pool will always be a reminder of the kindly thought which prompted their construction.

I will now ask Sheila Turner to present Mrs Lawrence with a bouquet."

On 30th January 1936, after the death of His Majesty King George V ten days previously, the then Lord Mayor of London set up a Committee to consider what form a national memorial to the King should take.

In March 1936, the Committee decided that there should be a statue in London and a philanthropic scheme of specific character which would benefit the whole country and be associated with King George's name. As a result, the King George's Fields Foundation was constituted by Trust Deed to give effect to the scheme. The Foundation, very much aware of the concept of a National Memorial, required security of tenure over the land and its dedication for more permanent preservation as a 'King George's Field'.

The aim of the Foundation was 'to promote and to assist in the establishment throughout the United Kingdom of Great Britain and Northern Ireland of playing fields for the use and enjoyment of the people. Every such playing field to be styled 'King George's Field' and to be distinguished by heraldic panels or other appropriate tablet, medallion or inscription commemorative of His Late Majesty and of a design approved by the Administrative Council.'

The Trust Deed defined a 'Playing Field' as "any open space used for the purpose of outdoor games, sports and pastimes."

At the opening ceremony leading figures were named as: W G Langley, chairman of Hathersage Parish Council who presided; Mr and Mrs G H Lawrence the donors; Sir Charles Clegg who declared the Field open; Alderman (Ald) and Miss Thraves, Lord and Lady Mayoress of Sheffield; J W Froggatt chairman of Outseats Parish Council; John Arthur Stead, Bakewell Rural District and Hathersage Parish councillor and Methodist Church warden; Mrs Peace, secretary Hathersage Memorial Council; Rev J H Brooksbank, Hathersage Vicar; G H Irvine, who seconded a vote of thanks; J A Strover, Head of Hathersage C of E School; Miss Sheila Turner, who presented bouquets to Mrs Lawrence, and to Mrs Moody of Charles Ross Ltd.

Before proceedings commenced fourteen years old Rachel Hudson, captain of the village school, stepped up to the microphone and proposed a vote of thanks to Mr and Mrs Lawrence for the children's amenities they had provided. Rachel still remembers what she said on that day: *"Sir Charles Clegg, Mr and Mrs Lawrence, Ladies and Gentlemen.*

As Captain of the Church of England school I have the honour of proposing a vote of thanks to Mr and Mrs Lawrence for their generous gift to the children of Hathersage.

The Sandpit and Paddling Pool will always be a reminder of the kindly thought which prompted their construction.

I will now ask Sheila Turner to present Mrs Lawrence with a bouquet."

Mr W G Langley, in welcoming the visitors, said that those of us who had been privileged to work with Mr Lawrence knew it had not been just an outpouring of wealth, but of the innermost soul of the man. He had been determined to give every facility in his power not

Above First swim in the new pool

only for this generation but also for the future.

In handing over the deeds of the Field to the Clerk of the Parish Council, Mr W J M (Billy) Bocking, Mr Lawrence specially mentioned Mr Langley, saying: "Hathersage is very fortunate in having such a man with such character and capabilities".

Mr J A Stead called GHL the "fairy godfather of the village".

After the opening formalities three divers, Joan Wall, Gwen Lindley and Muriel Fox, started the opening swim.

The official opening of the pool was reportedly on a glorious Saturday, the 25th July 1936, although the coats being worn by those present, as shown in photographs of the occasion, suggest otherwise.

436 spectators paid 3 pence each to attend.

Above and below Hathersage swimming pool 2010

The Sheffield City Police and Croft House Swimming Club put on a diving and swimming display, with several Sheffield and Yorkshire champions taking part, and they wound up their display with a water polo match.

The pool was opened for use by the public at 6 pm when 33 swimmers (other than swimming club members) paid 6 pence each to make use of it.

Leading players of the district played exhibition tennis games. On the Bowling Green local players took on a very strong team from Hallamshire Association. From the new Bandstand Hathersage Band provided music during the afternoon, and Holmes Mill Band then played during the evening.

GHL had also placed an order for 'Vulcan' cane café tables and 236 chairs with John May (Sheffield) Ltd of Arundel Street. Doubtless this gesture was prompted by his natural sense of loyalty to old friends and neighbours, for this John May Ltd was adjacent to 32 Eyre Street, where GHL had put in many years of strenuous business life.

Mr Lawrence ...'the fairy godfather of Hathersage'

The original estimated cost for carrying out the swimming pool works was in the region of £3,000. The final cost was reported to be about £6,500. (£350,000 after inflation, in today's terms). These figures exclude the cost of the site.

The Hathersage and District Swimming Club was formed on the inauguration of the pool, with GHL as President, and a committee consisting of:

H J Ratcliffe (Chairman), J Jepson (Vice Chairman), F R Cook (Hon Treasurer), Miss M C Mills (Hon Secretary), and Messrs J Bennett, A Chadburn, J Cave, G J Davis, J Jepson, J Pearce and Mrs A Smith. The club captain was G J Davis.

GHL had added a clause into the deeds forbidding games on a Sunday, "except swimming up to 10 am and concerts between 3 pm and 5 pm or after 8 pm". (This would avoid Church service times).

He is quoted as saying he did not want to be party to turning the field into a bear-garden on the Sabbath, and he did not believe the working class wanted Sunday games. To this end he had the playground equipment locked up on a Sunday.

Interestingly, in September 1936, at the end of the first season, a petition from villagers was lodged with the Parish Council asking this clause to be revoked. The Council then wrote to Mr Lawrence on the subject. There is no record of the outcome, or whether it was rescinded or amended. By April 1938 there seemed to have been a change of heart, when due to resident's complaints, the Parish Council chairman was going to discuss with Mr Lawrence, the possibility of preventing the Paddling Pool and Sandpit from being used on the Sabbath!

It could be argued that he had been right all along, for in 1944 it was suggested the amusements in the playing field should be locked up on a Sunday, and in spring 1946, Hathersage Parish Council considered steps to counter the nuisance created by weekend visitors to the playing field. A suggestion was made that an extra attendant should be appointed, so the field could be patrolled continually throughout the Sundays.

Another clause in the deeds forbade the property to be used for the holding of public meetings for the discussion of political or religious matters.

£10,000 for Lido:
"I wanted to use it in my own lifetime to do good to the greatest number of people." George Lawrence

☞ The Lawrence Hall

AS IF THIS WAS NOT ENOUGH for a man who also had a business to run, GHL decided in June 1936, while the swimming pool was being constructed, to build an extension to the Hathersage War Memorial building next door.

There had been a discussion going on for some time within the Memorial Hall committee, about obtaining a 'shed' that could be used as a gymnasium by the village. Now George Lawrence came along and offered to construct a proper building for this purpose. It was to be to a building plan satisfactory to him and to Mr Marcroft's verbal tender of £500 (£25,000) for the building 'shell', (i.e., floor, walls and roof, but not interior fittings and probably not lighting,

Lawrence Hall, Hathersage, 1936

heating or equipment etc). The cost to do this work today would be in the order of £50,000.

His offer was accepted and to deal with the matter the Memorial Hall committee appointed Messrs Hickinson, Mills, Cave, F R Cook, Frost, Scorah, Irvine, Langley, Holmes and the secretary to oversee the operation. Also co-opted were Mr W Clark and Mr Rylatt.

The work involved knocking down the existing outside toilets and a wall by the east end of the existing Stanage Hall. The Stanage Hall was then being used by the 'Men's Institute'.

This demolition work was then given to Mr Jackson and this new building was to be completed by C L Marcroft Ltd in just a month, that is by 25th July 1936, so that when the deeds were given to the Parish Council at the opening ceremony of the pool, the deeds for this hall could also be handed over to the Memorial Hall Council.

Mrs Peace, their secretary, duly received them with thanks on behalf of the Memorial Hall Council, and they included an extra piece of land to enable new toilets to be built, replacing those that had been demolished. The agreement being that the Hall Trustees were obliged to complete the toilets and they were then to be open to the public as they bordered onto the tennis courts, the car park and the swimming pool.

In the minutes of a Memorial Hall management meeting of 8th December 1936, occurred the first record of the new hall being referred to as the 'Lawrence Hall'. There appears to have been no formal resolution to this effect. It just came from a natural need to somehow identify the hall.

It was never officially dedicated to George Lawrence, yet remains the only enterprise in the village to carry his name.

At a meeting on 24th March 1937 mention was made of Mrs Lawrence's generosity as a result of her fund-raising efforts, then in April 1937 Mr Harry Schofield, the newly appointed head of the village school, was appointed to teach gymnastics in the Lawrence Hall.

Lawrence Hall extension expenses were eventually reported as £953, (£47,000) including the £500 given by GHL. There remained at the time an outstanding loan from Derbyshire Rural Community Council of £250 free of interest, to be repaid at £50 p.a.

Around this time GHL developed a desire to become a public servant. He unsuccessfully contested the Baslow division of the Derbyshire County Council when he was defeated by Mr P J Turner, but was elected in 1936 as a member of Bakewell Rural District Council (Bakewell R.D.C.).

He never stood for Sheffield City Council however, as he objected to party politics in municipal government.

For Bakewell R.D.C. he represented them on the Haddon Joint Hospital Board, on the Medical Officers of Health Joint Committee, on their 'penny-in-the-pound' Hospital scheme, and on the Peak Joint Planning Committee.

1936 marked the last time Sheffield United were in the FA Cup final, in the time of Ted Drake. They lost 0-1 to Arsenal. GHL was still a director and this was also the time when he paid for the first roof to be built over the Shoreham Street Kop terraces.

Hathersage Stanage Hall with the Lawrence Hall extension seen in lighter stone, 1936

1937

THE SWIMMING POOL water was originally unheated. However in 1937, GHL installed heating apparatus at a cost of £200 (£10,000 today) to keep the water at 68 to 70 degrees. Nowadays it rarely falls below 80 degrees (27°C). It was in May that same year that village school pupils first received swimming lessons, under John W Fellows.

GHL was very much a 'hands-on' individual. Not only did he provide the money and direction to see these projects through; he was also on the management committee which became responsible for the day-to-day running of the pool and hall and oversaw every detail, even down to providing towels for hire at the swimming pool, and brown paper bags in which to put ones' clothes, and hand them into the office for safekeeping.

A lot of future meetings of the Memorial Hall committee consisted of management items relating to Swimming Pool administration, as well as Memorial Hall matters. There appeared no demarcation between the two at this time and George Lawrence was very much involved with both.

Sheffield United football team treated by George Lawrence for a day out to Hathersage pool

At Bramall Lane George Lawrence who was known to all as the "Bladesman", it was said: "he might be considered more generous than his colleagues. ...and funded many a transfer out of his own pocket...."

He might well have helped buy the famous Jimmy Hagan who was bought from Derby County for £2,925 in November 1938.

For the United squad he would fund an annual, pre-season day out and dinner in Hathersage.

As a show of appreciation he gave an Armstrong Siddley motorcar to Ephraim 'Jock' Dodds, their Scottish international player, who was their highest goal scorer for five consecutive seasons from 1933 up to his transfer to Blackpool in 1939. He scored more than 110 goals for the club, and in his best season he netted 34. In those days football players did not earn much money and an Armstrong Siddley was one of the top cars. The footballers maximum wage was fixed in 1922 at £8 a week during the summer and £6 during the winter (£400 and £300 a week today) and remained the same in the 1930's, although Sheffield United paid only four of their twenty-one professionals this amount in the 1934/5 season.

George Lawrence became President of the Hope Valley Amateur Football League (HVAFL) and provided handsome trophies for this and for other local sporting organisations.

The trophy he presented to HVAFL in 1937 is 'The Championship Cup', played for to this day as one of the two main trophies. At the end of each season the four teams at the top of

the premier division play off for this trophy. The final is the last competitive match of the season, bringing down the curtain on the Hope Valley League competition. It is said that the cup is larger than the F.A. Cup and also cost more!!

Fittingly, the first season it was presented it was won by Hathersage Football Club who beat Birchover Football Club 4 goals to 3 in a thrilling match at Stoney Middleton.

The photograph here shows GHL presenting the cup to Hathersage skipper Norman Siddall, with Charlie Langley, Dennis Pearce, Mervyn Schofield and, behind, a young Bob Crookes also in the frame. Hathersage also won it the following year.

The output of Lawrence's factory never appeared to reach the two million razor blades a week suggested in the headline of the 1933 newspaper article, but in 1937 his works were turning out one million, going to all parts of the world. On the Laurel Works letterhead of 1938 there was a note that they were *Contractors to the Indian Army*.

Ted Flint, who became Lawrence's engineer in 1937, had started in the business of razors in 1933, working at J Stead & Co Ltd at Manor Lane, Sheffield, run by Alfred Stead and his younger brother John Arthur Stead, from Hathersage.

In those days, Steads made gramophone needles, 'Songster' record players, 'Vulcan' springs, typewriter springs, clock springs, springs for golf bags, governor springs for clockwork motors, springs for pocket knives, and razor blades.

Steads had made gramophone needles and steel pins since the 1880's at Victoria Mill, Hathersage, until its boiler blew up, when they moved to the Manor Lane Works.

Until he was 18, Ted Flint was educated at King Edward VII School, Sheffield. It was then by reputation the top school in Sheffield and was a public school when Ted first went there. In 1927 the Labour Council "downgraded it". The OTC [Officer Training Corps] was disbanded and in July R. R. Philips of William Ridgway & Sons Ltd (who became Master Cutler) took the passing out parade. On the same day the OTC was replaced by the formation of a Scouts troop.

Steads had started making razor blades in late 1932. It had been running six or seven months when Ted Flint started to work there. He had learnt his engineering skills at Sheffield University (part-time) and then picked up a lot more at Steads.

In 1937 he left that company to go to George H Lawrences, he said to replace GHL's brother-in-law, Percy Holmes, (although this name may not be correct).

When Ted arrived at Lawrences he said he had never "seen such a mess" in the grinding machines. He stripped one machine down to look inside it and found all the guides were useless. He made a drawing and went to see John Cooper & Son Ltd, the press-tool people in Garden Street, to make him some new ones.

He had the new guides within 24 hours, so on the Wednesday, when the machine was re-built, the operators said it was a treat to work on it, with everything being consistent all the time. On the first day, that one machine did as many as two machines had done before and there was hardly any scrap.

It was also around this time that GHL became aware of the enormous needs in Western Europe, still recovering from the effects of the First World War.

More than likely because of the friendship he had developed with Ald William Farewell Wardley of Sheffield City Council, a man about twice his age - he was encouraged to make generous donations to the French and Belgian war-devastated regions.

Much of his benevolent gestures centred around the town of Bapaume, in northern France, as a result of Sheffield Battalion's involvement in that area during the Great War.

Left Hope Valley Football League Championship Cup and seen presented by George Lawrence to Hathersage FC in 1937

Below G H Lawrence Ltd letterhead displaying its contract with the Indian Army

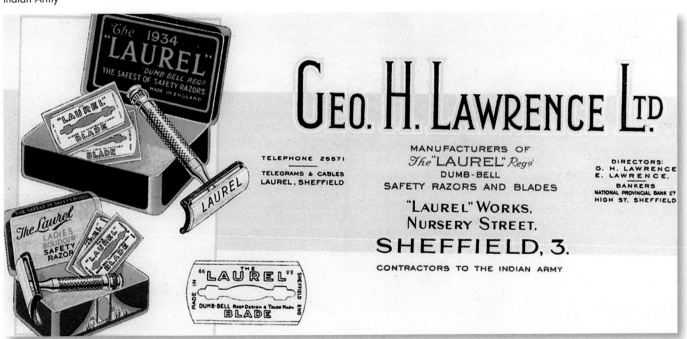

The Battle of the Somme

The last 140 years of the story of Bapaume seems to have been mainly one of war and devastation. During the Franco-Prussian War 1870-1871, the Battle of Bapaume was fought nearby on 3rd January 1871. The Prussian 1st Army had reached Bapaume at the end of the previous December, while at the same time the French Army of the North under General Faidherbe, moved out to break the German siege of Péronne. Although Faidherbe's green troops more than held their own against the outnumbered but experienced Prussians, they didn't follow up their advantage but instead retreated. As a consequence, Péronne surrendered on January 10.

During the period of the Great War (1914-1919) battles raged on and off for several years all around the town, which lies in the heart of the Somme. These areas in Northern France and Belgium were gradually and completely devastated.

Bapaume, was first occupied by the Germans on 28th August 1914, and became the British target to be retaken during the first days of the 'Battle of the Somme'. However this aim was not achieved and between July and September 1916 all of the population fled for their lives, not returning until 1919, to undertake the massive reconstruction then necessary.

1st July 1916 is remembered as the 'Battle of the Somme' and the day in World War One on which the greatest number of Sheffield men died in battle. The majority of the casualties were from the 12th Battalion, York and Lancaster Regiment (Y&L), known as the 'Sheffield Pals', although the official title was the Sheffield City Battalion..

German Kaiser Wilhelm II arrives in Bapaume on 14th September 1914

Among these would be trainee soldiers who bivouacked overnight in Hathersage School on Wednesday 24th March 1915, whilst on an exercise from their Redmires camp.

Sheffielders were also present in the makeup of 46 other units that fought on that first day of the Somme.

The British offensive had been designed to deal a tremendous blow to the enemy by driving his forces back towards the town of Bapaume and by doing this to give relief to Marshall Joffre's French troops at Verdun. It was to be the first major engagement of Kitchener's 'New Army' - a force of volunteers, untested in battle.

The Sheffield City Battalion and the 'Accrington Pals' - 11th Battalion of the East Lancashire Regiment were in the front line of the 94th Brigade, with the 13th and 14th Y&L, the 'Barnsley Pals', following them. Their role was to attack along a 700 yard wide front and to help to capture the village of Serre, half a mile away and lying just 16 km (10 miles) to the west of Bapaume. For several days before the attack, British artillery pounded the enemy's defences, trying to destroy the barbed wire protecting their front line and their heavily fortified dugouts and trenches. Delayed by two days of heavy rain, which left some British trenches half full of water, the attack finally took place on Saturday 1st July, a beautiful warm sunny day. There was concern that the element of surprise had been lost and the Germans were aware of the impending attack. Tapes laid by the British overnight to mark the safe paths cleared across no-man's-land and through the German barbed wire were removed in some areas, and as dawn broke on 1st July German artillery shelled British front line trenches.

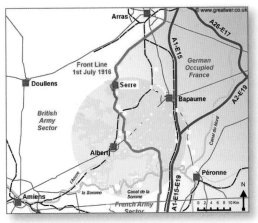

The Front Line between the German and Allied Forces at the commencement of the Battle of the Somme, 1st July 1916

Three hours later at 7.20 am the first wave of British troops 'went over the top' into no-man's-land and lay down in waiting about 100 yards beyond their own trenches. They were followed by a second wave a few minutes later.

The signal to attack came at 7.30 am. The British artillery barrage momentarily stopped, and in the few seconds of eerie silence following, the British troops advanced, line abreast - as if they were on parade. The Germans coming out of their largely undamaged dugouts constructed so deeply underground that the British shells failed to destroy them, hurled rifle and machine gun fire into the lines of advancing troops. The horror of the Somme was about to unfold. The German front line wire was found to be almost intact and this held up the attackers, allowing the enemy to pick them off, the few who reached it.

The attack stalled, and by 8.45 am it became apparent that the day was lost. The 13th and 14th Y&L, following up, were unable to get beyond their own front line.

It later appeared that small numbers of men had reached their objective in Serre and about 150 were reportedly holding their position in the German front line. Patrols were sent out in the early hours of 2nd July to try to establish contact but were withdrawn when wounded men were found who stated that any others in the German trenches had become casualties and were unable to offer any resistance. The only troops who reached Serre were those taken prisoner.

The last City Battalion roll call before the battle on 30th June, listed 36 officers and 980 other ranks. The next roll call, taken on 7th July, stood at 18 officers and 485 other ranks. 495 men were casualties of whom 201 were missing in action, the rest killed or wounded, and of the missing in action all but 18 were dead. In fact only 747 other ranks had gone into action on 1st July - giving a casualty rate of 66% - two out of every three men.

165 of the dead from the Sheffield Battalion were never identified and their names along with over 73,000 others are on the Thiepval Memorial commemorating all those killed in the battle of the Somme who have no known graves.

A combined tank and infantry attack at Bapaume

A surviving member of this battle, J Watson Jago, was later to become the local GP doctor for Hathersage and Grindleford for many years. The last survivor of the Sheffield Battalion was J R (Reg) Glenn who was a Lance Corporal during the Somme campaign, and was later promoted to Captain. He died in 1994.

Eventually in February 1917, the Germans withdrew strategically from Bapaume as they shortened their front to the new Hindenburg Line, and Australian troops occupied the town on March 17th 1917. However on 25th March 1917 a huge long-delay fused bomb exploded under the Town Hall, killing several soldiers and two prominent local politicians as well as completely destroying the building.

The Germans retook the town on 24th March 1918 and the New Zealanders freed it for the final time on 29th August 1918.

Bapaume in ruins

After the war, moves were made for various cities and towns in the UK to make themselves financially responsible for the restoration of some French areas, which had been devastated in the war. Many of the principal towns of Britain, France and America agreed to assist places in France and Belgium so affected. Already arrangements had been made with a shipping firm to carry donated goods at a very low freightage to where the French railways would take them on to their destination.

It was reported on 7th July 1920 that Sheffield's Lord Mayor, Sir Samuel Roberts, had been deputed to collect information on communities in France that Sheffield could 'adopt' in this way. Serre was particularly mentioned.

On 14th July 1920 under the presidency of the Lord Mayor, there was a public meeting of leading Sheffield citizens at the Town Hall, to consider a proposal to 'adopt' the township of Bapaume and the hamlet of Serre, with a view to helping to get them reconstructed and on their feet again.

The generosity of Sheffield people of all walks of life was to be solicited. The meeting constituted itself into a committee with the power to act, Captain Douglas Leng being elected secretary.

The Lord Mayor promised to visit the places and report back later, and on 25th July 1920, accompanied by his father Sir Samuel Roberts Bart., MP for Ecclesall, he visited Bapaume where he toured what remained of the town into which residents had started to return.

They were living in makeshift shanties made from rescued corrugated iron and timber from the battlefields. These communities were, however, denuded of furniture and implements and equipment necessary to restart their normal activities. He was told that articles of any kind, however useless they may be to people at home, would be extremely acceptable to the residents returning to these devastated districts.

The Mayor of Bapaume said that their task to transform the existing chaos was almost heartbreaking, but with Sheffield's assistance they were now hopeful, although there was much to be done that money could not replace.

The Sheffield party, accompanied by French representatives, then motored to Serre, where so many of the Sheffield Battalion lost their lives. Nothing remained to indicate it was once a hamlet of 150 inhabitants, its location known only by the stump of a huge tree. In the bright sunshine the spot was desolate.

Afterwards, local French representatives were invited to visit Sheffield and friendly relations afterwards continued between the two towns. Sheffield became the 'Godmother' of Bapaume and became known in Bapaume as her 'Mother City'.

The sum of £4,823 - 3 - 1d (£250,000) was collected from the Sheffield public, including £1,025 (£52,000) collected by a 'Sheffield Telegraph' appeal, but no contribution appears to have been made by the City Council. Of this sum, £1,166 - 12 - 11d (£60,000) was contributed by the children of Sheffield for the benefit of the children of Bapaume and Serre.

Immediately farming implements were purchased and gifts given to needy cases of the people and children of Bapaume. To Serre they gave a tractor and quantities of corn seed.

From the fund £3,200 (£160,000) was sent to the 'France : Grande-Bretagne Association', an organisation looking after the adopted towns.

The Ladies Committee, of which Ald Mrs Longden and Lady Hart were organizers, collected 2,500 articles of clothing, which were distributed in Bapaume.

Following Sir Samuel Roberts, Ald W F Wardley became Sheffield's Lord Mayor. He was the first Labour Party member to hold this office. Born in 1848 he left school before he was 10 when he joined his father at the anvil in the cutlery and forging trade. He became secretary of the 'Sheffield Table Blade Forgers and Strikers' Union'. He entered Sheffield City Council in 1890 where he specialised in questions affecting the public parks. For many years he was connected to Red Hill Wesleyan Church and supported all forms of sporting activities.

Sheffield became the 'godmother' of Bapaume and became known in Bapaume as her 'Mother City'.

During his Mayoralty of Sheffield (1921/22), he made the adopted French towns of Bapaume and Serre his charity which he then continued with thereafter. He also later became chairman of Sheffield Parks and Burial Grounds Committee, a post he held for several years.

Early in 1921 a local committee was set up in Bapaume, when it was announced that Sheffield intended to build some workers' housing, and Miss Stuart, on behalf of Sheffield, went to Bapaume to organise the distribution of funds.

In January 1922 Sheffield schoolchildren sent over warm clothes, sweets and cinema tickets. An hotel was built in Bapaume on Place de la Gare, opposite the railway station, in honour of the town's 'godmother', and called the 'Sheffield Hotel'. The building remains, but sadly is now only a warehouse, next to the restaurant "Le Gourmet".

A fifteen foot high monument built in the village of Serre, as a memorial to the men of the 12th Battalion, York & Lancaster Regiment, was unveiled on 21st May 1923 in the presence of a large contingent from Sheffield. It had been designed by J. S. Brown of the University of Sheffield, Department of Architecture. Money raised for this project included £213. 5s 4d (£10,740) in January 1923, from the Sheffield Telegraph appeal.

Ald Wardley was also chairman of the Sheffield-Serre Memorial Park Committee, which in August 1927 secured for 'all time' land for a separate Sheffield Memorial Park at Railway Hollow, near Serre. This was where the trenches had been, from which the Sheffield Pals and the Accrington Pals had gone 'over the top' on 1st July 1916.

Sheffield Pals Monument, Serre

The Committee had interviewed the landowner who had generously and patriotically consented to surrender possession of his property, provided that the Committee compensated the local French tenant farmer, which was done.

Four of the 'Sheffield Houses'

Through Ald Wardley's endeavours twelve 'Sheffield Houses' were built in Bapaume, financed by the donations from residents of Sheffield, each costing £500, a total of £6,000. (RPI increase =£300,000 today). The first tenants who occupied the houses on 15th September 1929 were intended to be selected as per category of need. Firstly, from First World War disabled, then war widows, then families living there before the war, and then war disabled or widows who had not lived in Bapaume before the War; but as there were far more applicants who qualified than there were houses, names were drawn out of a hat to decide who should first occupy them. These houses are still there, eight are on rue de Marcellin Gaudefroy and four are on the next street, rue de la Liberté. Today all are privately owned.

Owing to the Sheffield children making such a grand contribution, the Mayor of Bapaume (M. Guidet) promised that a crèche would be built at a later date and a sum of money was put aside for this eventuality.

The Sheffield-Serre Memorial Park and Shelter was opened on Whit Monday 25th May 1931. Inside the shelter was placed a stainless steel casket, given by Sir Robert Hadfield Bart., F.R.S., enclosed in a teak case with a glass front, made and presented by Messrs Walker & Hall Ltd of Sheffield. Inside was a roll of honour containing the names of all 4,898 Sheffield men who fell anywhere in the Great War whether in the air, on land or at sea.

The money raised by the committee for this purpose totalled £978, (£50,000) including proceeds of £248 (£12,500) from a football match between Sheffield Wednesday and Huddersfield in 1926, and £60 (£3,000) from the Sheffield Town Trust, and was given to the British War Graves Commission towards the cost of this Sheffield Monument. The Park was then vested in the Sheffield Corporation, who paid the War Graves Commission for its maintenance.

From 1922 and right up to 1939, the Sheffield and District branch of the British War Graves Association had organised annual pilgrimages to visit this and several other war cemeteries.

Some of the money collected by the committee was also used for the installation of a Memorial panel and a Roll of Honour in the Sheffield City (Memorial) Hall entrance in June 1935. This was designed by Mr John E Sunderland, the principal of the Sheffield College of Arts and Crafts, and made by his staff and pupils. The names of Ald Wardley and Mr J W H Smith (founder of Sheffield Branch of War Graves Association) will be remembered in connection with this.

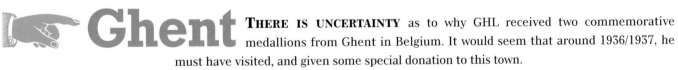 **Ghent** THERE IS UNCERTAINTY as to why GHL received two commemorative medallions from Ghent in Belgium. It would seem that around 1936/1937, he must have visited, and given some special donation to this town.

The specially printed banner accompanying the medallions he received reads:

To George Herbert Lawrence,
Renowned Citizen of Sheffield, Yorkshire, England
who by his generous benefactions has given proof
of his generosity of a singleminded purpose in well doing

The inscription on the reverse of the medals translates as:
"THE PEOPLE OF EAST FLANDERS RECORD THEIR PLEASURE. KING 1937".

It is known that similar medallions had been made available to the public for a 30 franc donation - which was really very little - to raise funds to replace statues of the reigning King Albert that had all been destroyed in 1918 by the retreating Germans.

A new statue was then erected, to King Albert I (1909-1934) and inaugurated in Ghent on 9th May 1937.

However the special banner made out to GHL suggests he had made a much higher contribution than 30 francs. Also this particular cause does not easily fall within the known parameters for his generosity, i.e., for the 'spiritual or recreational benefit of ordinary people'. Nor is there any evidence of his sympathy towards the Belgian monarchy, so the explanation of his 'benefactions' remains a mystery.

It is possible that at some time he visited the town on his way to Germany, from where he bought many of the machines for his factory, and while there, gave money for some other cause. The town then possibly used these readily available mementoes to recognise this? We just don't know.

We do know that Hathersage School went on a trip to Ostend and Ghent in August 1936, but there is no mention of him going with them or contributing to their expenses. We also know he did visit the town with the Sheffield Pilgrimage to France and Belgium on 13th July 1938, but this was after the date on the medallion and was after the statue had been finished and presumably paid for.

1937 statue to King Albert 1, Ghent

Medallions presented to George Lawrence from the people of East Flanders, 1937

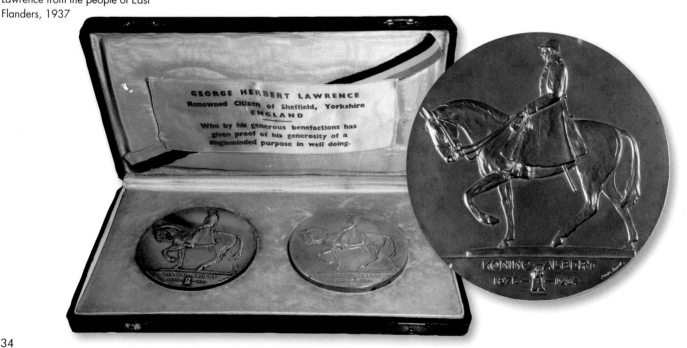

Hathersage

BACK IN HATHERSAGE, there had been talk for some years of the inadequacy of the existing Methodist Church, originally built in 1807. Even though it had been enlarged and a new facade had been put on in 1871. The building then straddled where the entrance of the drive to the present building joins the main road. It fronted onto the main road, and there was no footpath there at that time. Drunks and noisy motorbikes on the street caused considerable disturbance.

The original Methodist Wesleyan Chapel, Hathersage

In 1907 plans had been agreed for a new Chapel and Institute to be built on Castleton Road. This was previously the site of the old Atlas Mill (one of the five Hathersage mills). In 1906 this valuable site, together with all the building materials had been presented to the Church trustees,by Mrs Riggall, free of charge. I understand she was probably the wife of the Hathersage Minister at that time.

In spite of a 'petition' against this building scheme, work had been started on the Methodist Institute and Sunday school part of the project, the foundation stone for which being laid on 17th October 1907.

This building, which in 2011 houses the Nottingham County Council Environmental Education Centre was, during the 1914/18 war, taken over as an Auxiliary Red Cross Hospital for wounded soldiers, many of whom were Belgians, and then, later, many Australians arrived.

King George V and Queen Mary stayed overnight in the royal train at Hathersage station sidings on 28th September 1915 and invited any patients to visit them there, stipulating that they had to be there before 9.05 am! One wonders why he didn't take the trouble to visit the Hospital.

Design for a new Methodist Church and School or Institute, 1907 although only the Institute was built at this time *(right)*

The Royal train also stayed overnight at Hathersage station on 3rd May 1919, and again on 2nd June 1932 when the Prince of Wales (the future King Edward VIII) was going to Derwent. On both occasions the Hathersage school children went down to the station, to see the Royal train and hopefully catch a glimpse of the Royal personages.

The planned Chapel was not built at the same time as the Institute. It is thought that raising the money for the Institute and also for the new Manse, which had been constructed in Back Lane at the same time, was a heavy drain on the local Methodist finances. Then followed, after the First World War, the years of great economic depression.

However in 1937, Mrs Hancock put up for sale a large parcel of land behind the old, still existing Chapel. The Methodist Council voted 10 - 4 in favour of making this the location for the new Chapel instead of on the Castleton Road site, even though funds were still not available for the construction. However in December of that year, GHL generously made an offer of £5,000 towards the cost of the new Chapel as long as the remaining £1,000, required, was raised by other means. His offer was quickly accepted and finally things began to move and negotiations were quickly concluded for purchase of the land.

Joyce Woodcock recalls how GHL got up into the pulpit on that Christmas Eve, saying it was time to start building the new Church and he was going to give £5,000 towards it. She said he was quite 'well oiled' at the time.

John Arthur Stead said that although not actually connected to the Church, Mr Lawrence had attended a Methodist Church and Sunday school as a boy and now had warm regard for Methodism.

GHL had also wanted to build a hospital in the Hope Valley and said he was prepared to give £7,000 for it. (Inflation would make this £350,000 in today's terms, but one can imagine such a project would now cost upwards of £1 million). He said at the 1937 annual Bowling Club dinner that such a unit would have a maternity service, casualty wards and X-ray facilities.

He knew that, at the time, patients had to travel to Buxton or Sheffield for treatment, whatever the weather conditions.

Contributions from the existing 'penny in the pound' scheme locally represented £1,500 to £2,000 annually, which he suggested could be directed to the upkeep of his hospital. To this end he was prepared to increase the offer he had just made of £5,000 to build a new Methodist Church by a further £2,000 to build an adjacent Sunday School there, if he was able to take over the earlier Methodist Institute building for his proposed Hospital.

When the Sheffield Joint Hospitals Council Committee considered the proposal in February 1938, they turned it down, but with the possibility of a Maternity Hospital, which Derbyshire County Council were going to consider. However the idea proceeded no further.

Right The new Methodist Church, completed in 1939

1938

FOLLOWING ON IN 1938, Mr Brocklebank from Manchester was appointed as architect and W G Robsons Ltd were appointed building contractors, for the Church construction. Robsons were building the Williams Deacons Bank (now the Royal Bank of Scotland) and agreed to construct the Church soon after.

While these plans were being drawn up several other events were unfolding.

The friendship which developed between GHL and Ald William (Billy) Wardley, now chairman of Sheffield Parks and Burials Grounds Committee, resulted in him being invited to attend the April 1938 Outseats Parish Council meeting. This suggests he was a visitor staying with GHL at the time and probably the meeting was being held at GHL's 'Belmont' home. If this was the venue, it is something that Parish Councils are not allowed to do these days.

While there they were probably discussing another of GHL's projects, for on 25th May 1938, he agreed to provide a Swimming Pool in Longley Park in north Sheffield, almost identical in design to the Hathersage Pool. This time equipped with water heating.

The architect was Mr C G Jones of Syston, and the contractors were again to be En-Tout-Cas Co of Leicester.

Longley Park swimming pool, Sheffield, opened in 1938

Shortly afterwards, in July 1938, during the annual Sheffield Pilgrimage to France and Belgium, Mr W G Turner, chairman of the Sheffield Pilgrimage Committee, presented a gift from Mr G H Lawrence to the British Memorial School in Ypres, Belgium of a beautiful bookcase. It was 11' 6" long and 5' 9" high, designed and constructed by Messrs Swift & Goodinson Ltd of Sheffield. In thoroughly seasoned figured oak, having doors fitted with double diamond leaded-lights, it was made in four pieces for convenience in transit. Towards each end were carved two 'achievements' representing the City of Sheffield and the Company of Cutlers in Hallamshire. This work was designed and executed by Jack Clarkson A.R.C.A. of Sheffield College of Art & Crafts. Private individuals, business houses, ex-servicemen's organisations, police, schoolteachers and friendly societies from Sheffield supplied eight hundred and fifty books which were included with it.

British Memorial School, Ypres

FROM LATE 1918 the great task of clearing bodies from the Ypres battlefield and building the British cemeteries and memorials began. Initially military graves units did much of the work of bringing scattered burials from the battlefields into large consolidation cemeteries, until they handed over to the British War Graves Commission.

By the spring of 1919, a vast team of British ex-servicemen had been recruited to the work of creating and maintaining the new cemeteries. On the western front there were some 500 caretaker gardeners employed.

The Commission employees – gardeners, stone masons and administrators and their dependents – constituted a small but distinct community in and around Ypres.

Little by little, a 'British Settlement' was established, with its the church, grocer's shop and photographer's studio in a group of buildings erected in Ypres, at the corner of the Elverdingsestraat and the Vandenpeerboomplein.

Even so, if the parents wanted their children to have a British education, they had little option but to send their offspring back home. That is, until the British Military School opened its doors in 1929. Then for 11 years, it served as a beacon of British values, staffed by teachers from Britain.

In addition to the church and school, a chaplain's house and Pilgrim's Hall were erected on the site.

The old boys of one of Britain's most exclusive private schools, Eton College, supported the school.

Indeed, it was initially known as the Eton Memorial School. It was built with money raised by Eton College pupils who maintained a benevolent interest in it, as a living memorial to their 342 former school friends who perished in the Ypres Salient between 1914 and 1918.

It had another unique feature: it was attended almost exclusively by the working-class sons and daughters of the British gardeners who tended the WWI Imperial War Graves nearby.

With just four teachers and around 100 pupils, the school was famous as a showpiece for royalty and VIPs who visited Flanders Fields on pilgrimages and on every Armistice Day. At its height the school catered for about 130 students nearly all of them the offspring of Imperial War Graves Commission employees.

The bookcase and books donated in 1938 were therefore much appreciated by the staff, pupils and parents there.

Also during this same 1938 pilgrimage, Cllr Dr Froggatt promised the Mayor of Bapaume he would provide three sets of dental instruments for their clinic, "the best that Sheffield can make", and gave five guineas towards their clinic's funds. The Mayor gratefully accepted.

Another promise made the previous year was fulfilled. Ald Mrs Tebbutt made a gift to the Roman Catholic Curé of Hébuterne, (in whose parish the Sheffield-Serre Memorial Park was situated). This consisted of a pair of candlesticks for their altar, handsome reproductions of old Sheffield plate, suitably engraved.

Hathersage
Swimming Club
Championship Cup

In Hathersage it had previously been decided to erect memorial gates at the Back Lane entrance to the Playing Field, in accordance with the Foundation's intention that each scheme was to have an entrance designed to provide a sufficiently dignified setting for the heraldic panels that would distinguish the area as a 'King George's Field'. While no particular style was adopted by the Foundation, it discouraged indulgence in ornate or very expensive entrance gates.

On 17th September 1936 the Parish Council had asked if these gates were yet available for erection and eighteen months later a report in the Derbyshire Times on 11th March 1938 said that the design for the iron gates had been accepted by local councils and estimates of a cost of £300 had been submitted. The plans were with the King George's Fields' architect. However no record exists to suggest these gates were installed or even ordered.

In 1938 a silver Club Champion Cup was given to the swimming club by GHL and is competed for to this day at the annual Swimming Club gala. This is now awarded to the winner of a race of three lengths each of different styles. Each length starts from the deep end of the pool, with the competitors having to run back from the shallow end after each length.

He also gave a Junior Cup, which was won by Des Williams in 1938. Des also received a 12/6d 'Ingersoll' watch that year, again donated by GHL.

☛ Longley Park Pool

THE LONGLEY PARK POOL IN SHEFFIELD was officially opened at 3 pm on Saturday 3rd September 1938, by the Lord Mayor of Sheffield Ald E G Rowlinson after receiving it as a gift on behalf of the Citizens of Sheffield from Mr G H Lawrence.

At fourteen weeks from agreement to opening, this pool took only slightly longer to build than that at Hathersage, although it was not quite so extensive.

The Official Opening Party had proceeded by motorbus along with other members of the City Council and guests from the Town Hall.

Ald J Hewitt presided and Cllr H E Bridgwater thanked the Lord Mayor.

As part of the opening ceremony, Hathersage provided a junior dive team, got together by Stan Walker from the Hathersage Scouts. Miss Ivy Gill, who swam the English Channel in 1927, followed with a demonstration.

The pool was opened to the swimming public at 8 pm. Price of admission was 2 pence (40p today) including the cost of a paper bag and dressing box. Costumes could be hired for another 2 pence (deposit 2/6) and two towels could be hired for 2 pence (deposit 1/-).

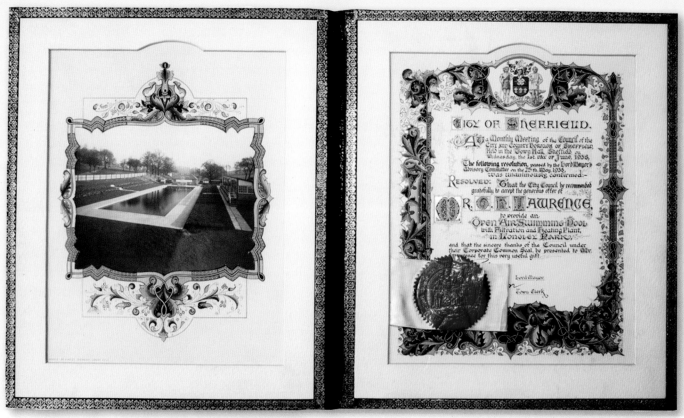

An illuminated book presented to George Lawrence by the City of Sheffield in recognition of his gift of the Longley Park Pool

The pool was designated to be open from 7 am to sunset in the summer and just from 8 am to 10 am in the winter (November to March inclusive).

In close proximity on the eastern side, the scheme again included a children's paddling pool and sandpit.

No mention has been found as to the cost of this whole project, but based on a 1979 estimate to replace it, the cost would be about £435,000 in today's terms.

The popularity of this venture can be judged from a report on 11th October 1938 to the Sheffield Council Parks & Burial Grounds Committee. This showed that the number of bathers attending Longley Pool during that first month of September was 13,315 compared with only 1,456 in Millhouses Pool.

During the first month 13,315 bathers attended Longley Pool

Mairie (Town Hall) in Bapaume

IN FRANCE Sheffield's intention to build a pre-school crèche in Bapaume had not yet been realised, but as one can see, there were many opportunities around at this time for Bill Wardley to tell George Lawrence that he was anxious to commence work on it. GHL must then have told him to go ahead with the matter and he (Mr. Lawrence) would give £500 (£25,000) towards the fund, because a Sheffield Council minute of November 1938 refers to "Sheffield's adopted city of Bapaume" and to "Mr Lawrence's generosity of £500 towards a crèche on land reserved between the houses given by Sheffield". His contribution was in addition to the £500 saved from that collected in the 1920's from Sheffield's children. To construct such a building today would probably cost in the order of £85,000.

Also in November 1938, GHL made surprise presentations in Hathersage to Mr W G Langley and Mr F Reg Cooke of a silver cigarette case each, in view of the tremendous amount of work they had done in connection with the King George's Field and Hathersage generally. As can be imagined, the various Hathersage projects must have involved a lot of work for others as well as for him, and these presentations by GHL were totally within his character.

At Lawrence's works, all the machines for making the double-edged blades were by this time supplied from Solingen, Germany. Fred Cam (Engineers) Ltd made the only Sheffield grinding machine they had. This was a single edge machine, which was later converted to grind the Ladies' blade. They also had a cartoning and packing machine made by Rose Brothers of Gainsborough.

They bought their carbon steel razor strip from Fox's of Stocksbridge, and from Rotherham Strip they also obtained carbon steel, which was used for all the cheaper blades. They also bought special steel strip from Sanderson Brothers & Newbould. This was an alloy of steel with nickel and chrome. It was rust-resistant and gave a better cutting edge.

Whereas the normal blades were produced for 1/3d a gross (before the war), they would produce the cheaper ones probably at 1/- and sell them to Woolworth at 6/6d a gross, who would then retail them at a penny each, or 12/- a gross.

Nearly a million blades a week were being produced, of up to 150 different names, each having its own distinctive wrapper.

Every Wednesday a thousand gross of blades (144,000) were despatched to Woolworths, their best customer.

Greenup & Thompson's supplied the labels and paper in which they were wrapped. Some of the cartons were made at Robinson's in Chesterfield.

Lawrences were experimenting with stainless steel blades in 1938, the strip for which they got from Sandviks of Sweden, but a blank cost a penny (12/- a gross) before any work was started on them.

They also produced a special ladies' 'Boudoir' razor, for shaving legs and under arms. The holders were gold-plated and the blades half the length of the standard (a quarter of the area of a normal blade), so they were a delicate job to produce.

In November and December 1938 as the political situation worsened, George's foresight prompted him to send his works engineer, Ted Flint, over to Germany, to see the manufacturer of his machinery and get drawings and spare parts that they wanted. A lot of the drawings Ted already had, because he had copied them when at Steads, who had some similar machines.

Ted brought a lot of things back with him from Germany and arranged for other things to be sent. Later the German manufacturers were stopped from sending any of their fitters to England to carry out repairs to any of their machines!

Mr Lawrence had actually managed to bring Mr Besançon, the designer of the patentee of these machines, over to England from Solingen. He then got him to work permanently at Lawrence's in Sheffield.

Ted Flint recollected how, when he was in Germany he witnessed the 'Brown Shirts' persecuting the Jews. They were smashing up the shops and setting them on fire, and knocking the people about in the street, where they would just leave them until a van came along. Then, if they were still alive, more or less throw them into it. These 'Brown Shirts' were not from the town where this was happening. They were brought in from outside the area.

Himmler's 'Black Shirts' were also doing similar things to Jewish residents.

He remembered one case: it was Christmas Eve he thought, when he had gone to visit an English friend. He was the commercial traveller for Walker & Halls, who had been in the Rhine Occupation Army in 1919 and stayed in Germany to teach English and had married a German girl. There was a commotion, so they turned out the lights and looked through the windows. There was a German dentist across the road whose wife was Jewish-German. They brought out all the dental equipment and all the furniture on to the street and set fire to it.

Gold plated ladies 'Boudoir' razor shown against a postage stamp of its time, to the same scale

42

1939

THE LAST SERVICE IN THE OLD HATHERSAGE METHODIST CHAPEL was held on 19th February 1939. It was then demolished and services were held in the Castleton Road Institute.

The foundation stones of the new chapel were 'laid' on 13th May of the same year. Inside the new Church vestibule is a panel listing the names of the twenty Church members who 'laid' foundation stones and of thirty-one children who 'laid' foundation bricks. It was in this way their monetary donations towards the building fund, were acknowledged.

Back at Lawrence's works, they also wanted grinding wheels from Germany, because no one in this country could make a wheel to 'satisfy' the edge of the razor blades. The Carborundum Company had tried but they were using silicon bonding. These were no good as they were 'burning' the blades. The German wheels were made from magnesite, which was very fine lava, crushed and ground and then bonded together. Ted bought and arranged delivery of about 150 of these wheels.

The last consignment of goods they received was towards either the end of May or the beginning of June 1939.

Fortunately another Englishman who was in the grinding wheel trade in Solingen, decided to come back to Sheffield before the war started. He set up the 'Star Works' in Boston Street, and was making the grinding wheels, under the name of 'Dibyco', that Lawrence's wanted.

Ted Flint went over to Germany yet again at Whitsuntide in 1939 to get some more spare parts. As soon as he arrived in Cologne, he was met at the station by his contact, Herr Jurgis, who said they were immediately going to go back into Holland and he would bring with him the things Ted wanted. They were not to sit together on the train, but would meet again in Utrecht after they had gone over the frontier.

This last visit to Germany was just prior to the final pre-war Sheffield pilgrimage to the French and Belgian Battlefields from 7th to 12th July 1939, organised by the Sheffield Branch of the British War Graves Association, chaired by W G Turner. The party of 122, included the Sheffield Lord Mayor: Ald William Joseph Hunter, Mr and Mrs Lawrence, surviving men from the old Sheffield Pals battalion, and, among others, two children from Abbey Lane Council School, as guests of George Lawrence and representing Sheffield School children. One being John Trickett of 14 Abbey Crescent, Beauchief and the other was Jean Revill of 84 Springfield Road, Millhouses.

On Sunday July 9th there was a special memorial service at the Sheffield-Serre Memorial Park where Cllr Harold S Gent, a member of the Sheffield Pals battalion, laid a wreath. Cllr Gent was quoted as saying that George Lawrence "used to do a lot of things on the quiet and took very little kudos for it".

The Sheffield-Serre Memorial Park, Railway Hollow cemetary

A visitor to this service of remembrance was the Curé of nearby Hébuterne who had come specially to thank Mr E A Beasley, the pilgrimage secretary, for returning the chalice which he had rescued from Hébuterne Church in 1915 and had then handed back after the war.

Later that day the 'Alderman Wardley Crèche' in Bapaume, built by the municipality of Bapaume with the money from Mr G H Lawrence and the children of Sheffield, was opened by Lord Mayor Ald W. J. Hunter.

It was intended to build this next to the 'Sheffield Houses' but in the event Bapaume municipality built the crèche a short distance away, on rue Jean Baptiste Lequette.

The building consisted of an entrance hall, waiting room and cloakroom, a large playroom, consulting room and toilets, and a playground. Upstairs was the Superintendent's apartment; whilst in the basement were the heating boilers, storage and electrical distribution equipment.

Plaques on the front of the building can still be readily recognised. One reads:

"This building has been built and furnished thanks to Mr and Mrs Lawrence's generosity and other inhabitants of the City of Sheffield."

The other with clasped hands translates as;

"SHEFFIELD-BAPAUME.

FOREVER FRIENDS. FOREVER CLOSE

9th July 1939"

The crèche was dedicated to William Farewell Wardley to commemorate his work on behalf of the devastated town of Bapaume and his association with it afterwards. Ald Wardley was not in this group visiting France as he was not fit enough to travel. He would have been 91 at the time, and he died two years later, in 1941.

There were also gifts presented of twenty-five chairs for the crèche. On the back of each chair, donated by relatives, was inscribed the name of a fallen Sheffield serviceman.

Box of engraved cutlery given to all Bapaume school children by Mr and Mrs Lawrence

Mrs Lawrence also furnished the crèche with a nurse's room, called the 'Lawrence Room', and 450 children, including a few Belgians, Italians and Poles, were presented with a set of engraved Sheffield stainless, knife fork and spoon in an embossed case, from Mr and Mrs Lawrence.

Six English children of the British War Graves Commission cemetery gardeners were included.

The Mayor of Bapaume declared "Reassure the people of Sheffield that the people of Bapaume will keep in her deepest heart a boundless gratitude towards her godmother, with whom she wishes to associate her generous benefactors, Mr and Mrs Lawrence, whose names will remain graven in the hearts of the people of Bapaume".

The Alderman Wardley crèche in Bapaume

The Swift and Goodinson table, casket and Sheffield Roll of Honour

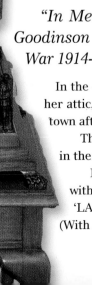

The Mayor was given a pocket-knife, similar to that given to the Duke of Kent when he opened the Sheffield Blackburn Meadows power station (demolished in August 2008). The Mayoress was given a case of four pairs of scissors, and pearl shafted pocket-knives were given to nineteen local Councillors and to the secretary. George Lawrence provided all these gifts. Mr W G Turner presented the Mayor with an illuminated address of thanks for the reception he had given the Sheffield Pilgrims, and Mrs Lawrence became the honorary president of La Bapalmoise, an organisation in Bapaume for the promotion of gymnastics among young girls.

Also presented from Sheffield, was a beautiful oak table and casket, which was installed in the Bapaume Town Hall. At its four corners the casket had sculptured bronze figures of soldiers standing with reversed arms and inside was a Book of Remembrance bound in blue Morocco leather with gold embossing:

"The City of Sheffield Roll of Honour to Sheffield men who fell or died of wounds in the Great War 1914-18".

In the book were all the names of the 4,898 Sheffield servicemen who died in the war. The list was hand-written by a member of the staff of the Sheffield Telegraph and Independent newspaper.

Table and casket were designed, constructed and given by Mr Maurice Swift and contained three books about Sheffield as well as the roll of honour.

On the front of the table is an inscription:

"In Memory of the Members of the Staff of Swift & Goodinson Ltd (Sheffield) who lost their lives in the Great War 1914-1918".

In the ensuing Second World War, a local woman hid the casket in her attic, in case it was destroyed, and she presented it back to the town afterwards.

This casket was later moved to one of the small upstairs rooms in the crèche, which became dedicated to the Great War.

Members of the Sheffield delegation were each presented with a medallion inscribed:

'LA VILLE BAPAUME RECONNAISANT 9 JUILLET 1939'
(With grateful thanks from the Town of Bapaume 9th July 1939).

Sheffield, and also GHL's help in France, were recognised as each was presented with a Sèvres vase by the Mayor of Bapaume. These were of beautiful design and colour, some 30" (75cms) tall. Unfortunately GHL's vase has now vanished. Perhaps he kept it at his office and it was destroyed when his factory was demolished in the 1940 blitz. Fortunately however, Sheffield's vase remains intact and is in the Town Hall to this day. There is a descriptive card with it which reads:

A Sèvres vase as presented to the City of Sheffield and to George Lawrence by the French Government

"This Sèvres Vase was given to the City of Sheffield and is a traditional ceremonial work which Bapaume obtained form the Secretary of State of France for National Education and Fine Arts. Such works of Art are specially designed and produced as gifts from the French President or members of the French Government; it is very difficult therefore to estimate its monetary value."

The French inscription on the base pays tribute to Sheffield as Bapaume's 'Godmother':

"LA VILLE DE BAPAUME RECONNAISSANTE A SA MARRAINE SHEFFIELD"

('Reconnaissante' = Grateful. 'Marraine' = Godmother)

On the same 1939 pilgrimage the party had earlier visited the British School at Ypres where, in the previous year, Mr Lawrence had given the beautiful bookcase.

On this occasion the scholars were presented by Lord Mayor Ald W J Hunter and Lady Mayoress Miss Hunter with a further 100 books provided by Mr M J Gleeson of Sheffield, for replacements and to keep scholars in touch with present literature.

In Hathersage George Lawrence was being referred to as its own 'Lord Nuffield'. Yet he was a jovial and convivial man who enjoyed life to the full.

Sir Charles Clegg who opened Hathersage Swimming pool and was "guided by the teachings of Methodism" was quoted as saying his hobbies were "the furtherance of temperance and football". George modelled himself on Sir Charles in many ways: he loathed gambling but, although followers of Methodism, both he and his wife liked their 'tipple', they did not 'sign the pledge', and they became well known in Hathersage for their drinking habits.

His wife, Elsie was a very good pianist and played at the Scotsman's Pack Inn on a Thursday evening when all present joined in the singing, many rendering their own solo 'party pieces'.She would often have a couple of drinks, bought by admirers, lined up on top of the piano. Albert Sunderland was the landlord there at this time.

Elsie's sister-in-law often remembered staying at 'Belmont' and sometimes coming downstairs late at night to find Elsie slumped in a chair, as she had been too inebriated to get upstairs to bed!

Several Hathersage locals remember how there were summer 'open days' at his 'Belmont' home, when any villagers could visit and wander round the gardens and have tea.

No one in need seemed to miss his attention, and he was quick to remember the poor people in the village, especially at Christmas time.

On Saturday 29th July 1939 Mr and Mrs Lawrence took a basket of choice roses and ferns to Mrs Alice Morton in her home at 'Barnfield' Hathersage, on the occasion of her 100th birthday. Her late husband had been the first Stationmaster at Hathersage from 1893.

Her celebrations included the Hathersage Silver Band who played under her bedroom window for over an hour in pouring rain. The Church bells rang out, and on the Sunday evening fifty members of Hathersage Methodist Church choir went and sang hymns to her. The music was relayed to her bedroom via microphone and speakers.

For his two sisters, GHL gave financial assistance to buy their own houses in Sheffield.

In the late summer of 1939 GHL arranged for a party of needy children from Hathersage to go and spend a week's holiday at Rossall Public School in Fleetwood, near Blackpool. It was at the time of Prime Minister Neville Chamberlain, for when the children returned to Sheffield it was 'blacked out'.

Then after the outbreak of war in 1939, and because no further supplies of coke or coal were available for heating, the Hathersage pool was declared closed on 30th September, with the proviso that any members of the Swimming Club could still use the unheated water.

George Lawrence - a jovial and convivial man

In Hathersage George Lawrence was being referred to as its own 'Lord Nuffield'

GHL was a member of the Razor Blade Manufacturers Association, of which Thomas Watkins Ward of 'Wardonia' was chairman. The Association dealt with the Board of Trade during the war to agree quotas of steel for their production.

Hathersage volunteer Fire Brigade had been formed in 1933 under the captaincy of J H Jepson, but had only basic equipment. Local Hope Valley villages had assistance from Sheffield, Buxton or Chesterfield for more serious situations, for which service the County Council paid these brigades a retainer. These other brigades however could take anything up to 45 minutes to attend a Hope Valley incident and George Lawrence was concerned that if enemy bombing caused a fire, a distant Brigade might be too occupied to help. In 1939 therefore he arranged, through Sheffield Fire Brigade, to buy a Coventry Climax trailer fire pump for use by the Valley. The reported cost was £230 (say£10,000). The Hathersage Brigade was then to be reconstituted and have its member numbers added to.

In October 1939 Walter Gosling towed the tender behind his car, back to Hathersage, where it was kept, first at Mr Rampley's garage in Barnfields, and in 1943 in the Nissen hut which the Fire Brigade was to occupy near the Parish Room. In 1962 it moved into what is now the permanent village fire station.

Above War-time advertisement encouraging greater self-sacrifice

Right A Coventry Climax trailer fire pump donated to Hope Valley by George Lawrence pictured with Mr Rampley, left, and Walter Gosling, centre

In 1939 GHL arranged to buy a new fire pump for use in the Hope Valley

Because the construction of the Hathersage Methodist Church was so far advanced at the beginning of the war, permission was granted for its completion.

It had also been realized that the organ from the old Church could not be used in the new one as intended, so Mrs Lawrence offered to defray the cost of an organ for the new premises. The organ was made by Mr Albert Keates, organ builder, of 86 Charlotte Road, Sheffield, and cost about £800. (£38,000 today).

Joe Ollerenshaw defrayed the cost of the electric lights using, where possible, the equipment he had only recently provided in the old Church in memory of his wife.

The Church was then officially opened on Saturday 30th December 1939 and Mrs Lawrence herself played the first hymn on the new organ.

The official opening party consisted of Joseph Ollerenshaw - who opened the Church; Mr and Mrs Lawrence; Rev Leonard Simpson - Hathersage Methodist Minister; Mr A Brocklebank - Architect; Mrs W G Robson - Builder; J Arthur Stead, Senior Methodist Circuit Steward; V Roche; Rev H J Watts - Chairman of Stoke and Macclesfield Methodist District; Rev E Benson Perkins; R Whitworth - Organist; Rev L Skinner - Tideswell Methodist Minister; Rev Baines Atkinson - former Hathersage Minister; Ald and Mrs J A Longden - Lord Mayor and Lady Mayoress of Sheffield; and Rev A Williams Boote - Bakewell Methodist Church.

TIMES, FRIDAY, JANUARY 5, 1940

Derbyshire

NEW CHURCH OPENED

Historic Day For Hathersage Methodists

GROUP TAKEN AT THE OPENING

Front (left to right): **Mr. G. H. Lawrence** (gave £5,000), the **Lady Mayoress of Sheffield**, **Mrs. Lawrence** (gave organ), the **Lord Mayor of Sheffield**, **Rev. Baines Atkinson** (formerly minister at Hathersage) and **Rev. L. Skinner** (Tideswell).

Back (left to right): **Rev. A. Williams Boote**, **Mr. J. Ollerenshaw** (who opened the church), **Rev. L. Simpson** (minister at Hathersage), **Mr. A. Brocklehurst** (architect), **Mrs. Robson** (builder), **Rev. E. Benson Perkins**, **Mr. R. Whitworth** (organist), **Mr. J. A. Stead**, **Mr. V. Roche**, **Rev. H. J. Watts.**

Saturday was a "Red Letter" day for Methodists in the North Derbyshire Circuit, and particularly Hathersage, where the opening of the new £6,600 aisles. Among the congregation were the Lord Mayor and Lady Mayoress of Sheffield (Ald. and Mrs. A. J. Longden). The organ was declared open by its Committee. He said he had been interested in the project from the start, for he was chairman of the district when it was launched. As secretary to the Chapel Committee he brought them

During the following day, on 31st December, each Sunday school child was presented with a Bible and hymn book, a further gift from Mrs Lawrence, who had also bought the Church 100 new hymn books for use by visitors.

It was stated, "because of the wish of Mr and Mrs Lawrence there was no tablet in the Church commemorating their gift".

An illuminated book, was presented to the Lawrences by Mr J A Stead, and is now displayed in the vestibule. After their deaths, in the 1970's, the family found the book and gave it back to the Church. It reads:

FROM MEMBERS AND FRIENDS OF
THE METHODIST CHURCH, HATHERSAGE, DERBYSHIRE.
GEORGE H LAWRENCE ESQ.

We wish to express to you our deep sense of gratitude for your most generous gift in the erection of the Methodist Church at Hathersage.
We greatly appreciate not only your munificence, but also your unfailing and enthusiastic interest in every detail of the scheme.
We also desire to record our heartfelt thankfulness to Mrs LAWRENCE for the gift of the organ, which will greatly enhance the beauty, and utility of the Church.
To be privileged to worship in a beautiful church such as you both have made possible fills our hearts with joy and thanksgiving.
MAY GOD USE YOUR GIFTS FOR HIS GLORY AND BESTOW ON YOU HIS RICHEST BLESSING.

This book was presented to Mr and Mrs George Lawrence in recognition of their generous gift, which enabled this Church to be built.

In the book is the Ceremonial Key which was used by Mr Joseph Ollerenshaw to open the church on 30th December 1939.

There is now also another plaque by the organ in the Church:
'To The Glory of God To Help in the Reverent Praise of God and in Gratitude for Blessings Received This Organ was Given by Mrs G H Lawrence Dec 30th 1939.'

The final cost of the building project came to £6,852 - 3 - 10d, excluding the cost of the organ. (RPI increase would make this £330,000, but it is more likely to cost some £425,000 today). In July 1941 an appeal leaflet issued by the Church showed that, apart from gifts promised, they required only a further £160 to clear the debt on their new Methodist Church.

Far right Interior view of Hathersage Methodist Church showing the organ, the illuminated book and memorial window

50

1940

IN FEBRUARY 1940 THE METHODIST INSTITUTE on Castleton Road, Hathersage, was again requisitioned for use by the military, before becoming a satellite war production factory of Marsh Bros from Sheffield, a Small-Toolmakers.

The Hathersage swimming pool was also requisitioned and an Army Artillery Battalion was posted into the village and used the pool and the buildings.

In this same month of February 1940 GHL handed over, via Sheffield's Lord Mayor, Ald J A Longden, a draft for 500,000 French francs, (about £5,000 or around £250,000 in today's money), as half the amount he had promised to the French Reconnaissance Committee (the French 'Foyers du Soldat').

In acceptance the Lord Mayor said GHL was also looking after our own soldiers here in Britain. Time and again he made generous contributions towards funds for their welfare.

The French gift was shared between two sister charities of the French YMCA, who provided social clubs, mobile canteens, libraries and other home comforts for their troops. GHL stipulated these clubs should recognise the contributions were from 'Sheffield' and not from him personally.

The remaining half of his promised gift was to be handed over during the summer of 1940 so as to provide wool for garments for the French troops during the following winter's campaign, but France capitulated in June 1940 and so this money was never donated.

GHL did, however, send a week's production of 1,000,000 razor blades to the French troops. The value to him in lost sales was over £100,000 in today's terms.

The French government and several charities recognised his generosity in letters he received from: Édouard Daladier, the French Prime Minister; M Corbin, the French Ambassador in London; Madame Louise Thuliez, the President of Foyers du Front; Madame the Marquise du Polignac, the President of Foyers Mobiles du Soldat, (and wife of General Georges, the Commandant in charge of French war operations in the North East).

LES FOYERS DU SOLDAT
Y.M.C.A.
UNION FRANCO-AMERICAINE

GHL sent a week's production of 1,000,000 razor blades to the French troops. The value to him was over £100,000 in today's terms.

In the First World War Madame Louise Thuliez had been a collaborator of Edith Cavell, who was executed as a British spy by a German firing squad in Brussels on 12th October 1915.

Edith Cavell, the daughter of a Norfolk curate, was a nurse who became Matron of the first Belgium training school for nurses. In 1914 many war casualties came every day to her clinic, in occupied Brussels, and she and others helped some 200 Allied soldiers escape to safety before she was betrayed.

King George V and Queen Alexandra attended her funeral service in Westminster Abbey in May 1919, before her body was taken to Norwich Cathedral for re-burial. There is a marble statue to her in St Martin's Place, London, and a mountain was named after her in Canada. Such was the outcry at her death that the German Kaiser decreed that no other woman would be executed unless he personally authorised it.

Mme Thuliez was awarded the OBE.

Back in Hathersage the military de-requisitioned the swimming pool and buildings on 20th April 1940, but continued using the tearooms (now the Pool Café). This was only after the Battery Commanding Officer had insisted that his men returned to the pool towels that had disappeared during their tenure. Thirty-five were recovered.

The pool was then reopened to the public in the summer of 1940, and the Army was given permission to use it, providing they brought their own towels!

In May 1940 George Lawrence had decided to provide a motor ambulance for the use of Hope Valley residents. This was delivered to Hathersage on 26th and he agreed to maintain it for the duration of the war. (A similar vehicle equipped only to the simpler specification applying at that time would probably have cost about £30,000 today).

By May 14th 1940, after much bombing, most of the inhabitants of Bapaume had once more left the town which, on the 20th May, again became occupied by German troops. It remained under their control until September 1944.

On May 25th 1940 the Sheffield Telegraph and Independent newspaper describes how two English sisters and their husbands had been the last civilians forced to flee from bombing of the area. Mr and Mrs C Smith and Mr and Mrs T H Opie, had run the 'Prince of Wales' café at Thriepval, where the Sheffield pilgrimage party had lunched in 1939. They had left a cellar full of champagne and English beer, and faced bombing and strafing on their way to the coast, where they were rushed onto a hospital ship for the crossing to England. From there they travelled to the ladies' other sister who lived in Grindleford.

During the war GHL and his wife Elsie were very active in supporting various fundraising activities. No Sheffield charity ever seemed to appeal to them in vain, and often they assisted anonymously. He was often quoted as saying, "I made my money in Sheffield and Sheffield shall have the benefits of it".

Among many others, the Sheffield Newspapers 'War Fund' repeatedly gained from his donations. On a number of occasions he doubled the proceeds of concerts and other events arranged in aid of the fund. One such example was after a concert held at the Regent Theatre in Barkers Pool on 1st May. This made a profit of £113 - 15 - 8d (£5,500 today) and GHL in accordance with his promise gave a cheque for a similar amount.

He played a prominent part in the promotion of Millhouses and other 'cricket weeks' for this same War Fund. His wife also supported the Mistress Cutler's ANACA Fund.

He arranged snooker matches for the Red Cross between Tom Reece and Melbourne Inman and between Sidney Smith and Tom Newman.

When the Bakewell Services Recreation Club required an extension to their premises he very readily gave £100 (£5,000).

For several years he had always defrayed the cost of the band at the annual dances in aid of the Derbyshire Constabulary Widow and Orphans fund.

He met the expenses of the Bakewell & District Fighter Fund and he was chairman of 'Baillie' Hospital Bowls Competition (for the benefit of Bakewell and District Cottage Hospital).

The Blitz

GEORGE LAWRENCE'S UNTIMELY DEATH was all the more tragic as it occurred when he was doing what he had always advocated, namely looking after others he considered less fortunate than himself.

He was killed in the first major Sheffield blitz of the Second World War, on the night of the 12th/13th December 1940.

On Thursday 12th the early air raid warning 'code yellow' came though to the local Sheffield control stations at 6.15 pm, suggesting an attack was likely, but without the assurance that Sheffield would be the target. This had turned to 'code purple' by 6.45 pm when all local organisations were alerted, becoming 'code red' when the sirens were sounded at about 7 pm. Bombs began to fall soon afterwards. There was a full moon and the ground

The Sheffield Blitz at its height, December 1940

and roofs were white over with frost, making it perfect weather for the raiders. It was said there were about 300 aircraft used.

The worst part of the attack came between 11 pm and 1 am. The 'all-clear' was sounded at 4.17 am on the Friday morning, 13th December.

GHL's engineer, Ted Flint, recalls that on that night when the 'purple' signal came through he had urged the people on the ground floor of the works, to pack up and go home, and they all did.

The packing department stayed, and when the sirens sounded they all put on their coats and made for the Works' air-raid shelters. Some went into their new shelter and several into the Caretaker's shelter. Elsie and John Berrisford, together with Arthur Hessey, (the Caretaker), with his wife Edith, Fred Davies, (the Electrician) and many more were in the Caretaker's shelter when the bombs were dropping. The electrician suggested they should all go to the new shelter, which was in the basement of the building in the front, so they all joined hands in a 'chain' and rushed for it.

It could be said GHL had no right to have been in Sheffield at all that night. He was in Hathersage when the air raid started and he became concerned for his staff in the packing department, who were working until 8 o'clock that evening. As he couldn't contact them on the telephone, he decided he should go to them.

The local Hathersage policeman, Ron (Rip) Kirby, stopped GHL by the Ordnance Arms public house in the late evening, and tried to prevent him going to Sheffield. However he would not heed Ron's warning, who said "he had had one or two". One might think he may have needed some 'Dutch Courage' to do what he did that night?

He then called at the Scotsman's Pack Inn, where locals also tried to persuade him not to go, but he insisted he must, and he bought four bottles of whisky to take with him along with food he had brought from his home.

After an earlier air raid on Sheffield, Winnie Roadknight and several Hathersage Church ladies had made soup for the people from Sheffield, but only two had turned up. The remaining soup was taken by GHL to his works that night.

The Sheffield police stopped him yet again at Dore Moor Inn, on the outskirts of Sheffield. They were stopping all the traffic from going into the town, but he insisted on continuing. Then, even before he arrived at his factory, he had picked up a wounded soldier and two civilians and taken them to hospital.

He parked his car in Johnson Street at the side of his works' despatch entrance and went down into the new shelter with the provisions he had brought. Shortly afterwards Elsie Berrisford suggested they should kneel down, whereupon she offered a prayer, and many joined in.

Bomb damage to Lawrence's Works, Nursery Street

Incendiary firebombs had been dropped first, and they set Wood's timber yard alight next-door.

Then bombers came along and dropped a string of high explosive bombs, one on the timber yard, one a bit higher up near the mortuary, and one that hit the back of works where the grinding machines and polishing machines were.

Then early on Friday morning 13th Dec, GHL, Fred Davies and the Caretaker had been out of the air-raid shelter and up the staircase, looking out of the despatch doorway to see what was happening. They were on the way back down when the fateful bomb landed. Fred Davies, the electrician, was half way up the staircase. He was got out alive on the Friday, but he suffered from internal injuries and died on the Sunday in the Royal Infirmary. He had seemed all right and was talking to Ted Flint as they cleared the debris away to get him out, but there were so many injured people in the hospital that night that they must have had tremendous difficulty coping with them all.

George Lawrence was lower down the stairs and his body was found on the Sunday, but they couldn't find the Caretaker. He was eventually found a fortnight later, near to the door. He had been locking the door and was laid over some packing cases, which were ready for despatch.

An article in the Saturday's 'Star' newspaper reported how Mrs Lawrence had not heard from her husband since he went into Sheffield, although a man recovered from the wreckage told her that GHL was standing next to him at the time. A similar report was in the Daily Express on Monday 16th December.

The Roll of Honour compiled by the Imperial War Graves Commission, of people who died in Sheffield from the enemy action that night, listed the nine who died at the Nursery Street works early on 13th Dec. It included George Lawrence and two men with both of their wives.

One couple, Elsie Winifred and John Redfern Berrisford (both age 33), were living at the time in Lawrence's old house at 83 Southgrove Road. The other couple, Arthur Hessey (39) and his wife Edith (38), were of 25 Horner Road.

Bramall Lane football ground which was hit by ten or eleven bombs

Also killed were Florence Coverley (30), of 53 Upwell Street; Frederick William Davies (47), (Electrician) of 34 Springhouse Road, Crookesmoor; Madge Green (24) of 10 Grimesthorpe Road; and Nora Kendall (23) of 20 Belper Road.

The list was published in "Sheffield Blitz", a book produced by Sheffield Newspapers Ltd and was, after the Marples Hotel disaster, probably the second equal highest death total in any single incident of the raid, together with the Porter Street Shelter.

The workers from the nearby Bridgehouses Railway sidings came after the raid had finished and got out the rest who were still alive.

Margaret Majkut of Hathersage recalled seeing the completely ruined factory shortly afterwards, when coils of shiny razor blade steel strip had been blown out and festooned itself round the pinnacles of the tower of the next-door Holy Trinity Church and the works. The effect was quite dramatic, and being so near to Christmas it made a very macabre memorial to a man with a heart of gold.

In the same air raid, ten or eleven bombs were dropped on Bramall Lane football ground destroying a large part of the John Street stand and the roof GHL had had built over the 'Kop'. There were at least two craters on the pitch itself. Bombs also fell on the "popping creases" of the cricket square. Sheffield United football team were then forced to play at Sheffield Wednesday's ground at Hillsborough until Bramall Lane was patched up for the following 1941/42 football season.

MR. G. H. LAWRENCE

Death of Mr. G. Lawrence

Telegraph & Independent 16 Dec. '40

Sheffield Raid Victim

Mr. George H. Lawrence, the Sheffield industrialist and generous supporter of local charities, was among those who lost their lives in Thursday night's air raid. He went to a building in the city which was hit. His body has been recovered.

Mr. George H. Lawrence's career was a romance of industry. He rose from a seller of "The Star," running miles each night to earn a few pence, to be the head of one of Sheffield's most thriving razor blade businesses, and a man whose generosity embraced not only his native city but other towns and countries.

Ironically, on Thursday December 19th 1940, for his funeral, his body was the first ever to be brought into the Hathersage Methodist Church, which he had ensured had been built and opened just twelve months earlier.

Those attending his funeral included his father, and upwards of sixty of his workforce who arrived in two motor coaches; the Lord and Lady Mayoress and the Deputy Lord Mayor and Lady Mayoress of Sheffield and the Mistress Cutler, and representatives from various councils and sporting bodies he was associated with, freemasons lodges, businesses and charities.

There was then a memorial service to him in the same Church on Sunday 29th December, twelve months to the day after he and his wife had presented a Bible and a hymn book to every Sunday School scholar to mark its opening.

George Herbert Lawrence died intestate, but when probate was granted on 21st July 1941 his estate was valued at £29,484 - 7 - 7d gross, £26,268 - 12 - 7d net, which, in 2011, equates to about £1,500,000.

Above Geoge Lawrence's funeral was the first to be held in the Methodist church he had built just a year earlier
Right His grave in Hathersage Parish Churchyard

IN MEMORY OF
GEORGE HERBERT LAWRENCE
KILLED IN ACTION 13TH DEC. 1940 AGED 52 YEARS
HE DIED AS HE LIVED SERVING OTHERS
ALSO OF HIS BELOVED WIFE
ELSIE
PASSED AWAY 11TH DEC. 1946 AGED 57 YEARS

"A man of few words in the chamber but of deeds in the district."

Elsie

THIS BED IS ENDOWED
IN PERPETUITY BY
ELSIE LAWRENCE.
IN MEMORY OF
HER BELOVED HUSBAND
GEO. H. LAWRENCE.
A GOOD CITIZEN & BENEFACTOR
OF THIS CITY OF SHEFFIELD

A plaque to one of the beds
endowed in three Sheffield
hospitals

Tributes followed. At a Bakewell Rural District Council meeting, where he had been a member for four years, he was described as 'a man of few words in the chamber but of deeds in the district'. It was decided to ask the joint Parish Councils of Hathersage and Outseats to nominate a successor to the council.

THROUGH HER GENEROSITY MRS ELSIE LAWRENCE, his widow, made sure the poor in Hathersage were not forgotten that Christmas, as she assumed the mantle of benefactor in his place. Yet the emotional, social and financial implications for her must have been tremendous.

Not only did she have the problems associated with her sudden bereavement but she immediately became Chairman of George H Lawrence Ltd, having the responsibility of the re-housing of the works and its staff. With her husband she had owned the company jointly with her husband, and she had taken a prominent part in founding it from rock bottom.

Ted Flint, now her engineer, told how they were toiling seven days a week after Lawrence's factory had been bombed, as they moved into part of A Scott (Duride) Ltd's factory, in Green Lane Works. The company had taken over two floors of the premises on the riverside, going down to Kelham Island Weir.

They gradually moved all the equipment out of Nursery Street and got set up, but it would appear that they continued to use part of their old offices, as their postal address remained there. Of all the machines recovered from the damaged works, one that had its back broken was repaired by 'stitch' welding it at Daniel D Doncaster's Ltd. The Cam's machine was not worth bothering with.

After full production was resumed, practically all the output was sent out to service personnel.

In her husband's memory, Elsie Lawrence endowed a bed at each of the Royal, Royal Infirmary and Children's Hospitals in Sheffield, and three years after his death, on 27th December 1943, she added to the Hathersage Methodist Church the beautiful stained glass window of 'The Good Shepherd', designed by Mrs Nevison.

On 4th January 1945 Elsie married Percy Bradley Johnson, at the same Hathersage Methodist Church. Before she would marry him, Percy changed his surname to 'Lawrence', apparently at her insistence. He was himself a widower with one son, but he and Elsie did not have any children together.

Percy Bradley had been a good friend of George and he too was well known in Sheffield sports circles. He had been a departmental manager in George H Lawrence Ltd and he now became a director of the company.

After the War, following a visit on government business to Bapaume, which had been liberated by the Americans on 1st September 1944, Mr John Burns Hynd, MP for Sheffield Attercliffe (1944-1970), passed on to Sheffield this message from the Mayor of Bapaume:

"The people of BAPAUME were deeply touched by the visit of the Member for SHEFFIELD, Mr. JOHN HYND, and therefore wish to express their real gratitude for what he has done. Mr. HYND also expressed his keen sympathy for their sufferings.

Remembering the 9th of July 1939, the town of BAPAUME would welcome a second pilgrimage by the people of SHEFFIELD in order that they may be able to express their gratitude personally to the town that has adopted them.

(Signed) Léonce Verdet." (Mayor)

John Hynd added his own note:

"I must say that the great friendship has been strong between Sheffield and Bapaume and I feel that this kind of friendship is good for both nations.

I propose to visit Bapaume early in 1946 and if this meeting feel so disposed, and a small Committee appointed, I will endeavour to arrange another visit from this City and renew the friendship which existed before the war.

May I say that most of the furniture of the crèche provided by Citizens of Sheffield, each in memory of a fallen relative, was taken away by the Germans and I have received intimation from many donors that they desire to replace their former gift".

1946

THESE SENTIMENTS WERE REWARDED, for Sheffield sent a delegation to France in May 1946. They were given special facilities at almost every stopping place en route through Belgium and France.

With the coming of World War II and German occupation, most of the British community had fled from Ypres; but at the British School, the 'Lawrence' bookcase and most of the books did survive, as the 1946 Sheffield Pilgrimage discovered when they visited. This was due to the caretaker's daughter Miss Joan Collick. She originally attended the school and when she returned from Cornwall in 1945 she immediately set about the task of recovering the books. The bookcase had been hidden during the German occupation, under rubbish in the attic of the Vicarage.

Unfortunately as there were hardly any British children who would attend the Memorial school after the end of the war, it was not resumed.

Rockets signalled the delegation's arrival in Bapaume and the whole town was gaily decorated. Bapaume's Mayor, M. Léonce Verdet, said that the bond of friendship between Bapaume and Sheffield would never be severed, though it had been interrupted for seven years. Pictures of the Sheffield delegation's visit to Bapaume appeared in the Sheffield press on 28th May and showed a band of French ex-servicemen and members of pre-service units,

The majority
of her
possessions
she left in
trust with
instructions
for them to
be used "in
establishing
objects of
charity and
benevolence"

youth organisations, with 800 schoolchildren, marching through Bapaume, where they paraded past the Sheffield visitors, including Mr J B Hynd M.P., and Mrs Hynd, and The Lord Mayor and Lady Mayoress (Ald & Mrs C W Gascoigne).

Bapaume's population had by this time been restored to some 2748 inhabitants.

The Lady Mayoress laid a wreath at the Sheffield City Battalion war memorial in Serre, but at the Sheffield Cemetery and Memorial Park it was reported that although the Germans had respected the graves during the hostilities, some deterioration had taken place. All members of the War Graves Commission had been interned except Mr Leech, the gardener, who was allowed to carry on caring for Sheffield Memorial Park, and Sheffield had him to thank for the safekeeping of the Sheffield Memorial Casket and Roll of Honour, from the shelter there.

Mr Leech also helped save seventeen Allied Airmen. He kept them hidden and fed in the cemeteries and tool sheds.

After the war the casket was taken to the Mairie of Puisieux-Serre where it was kept for many years. It now resides in the Museum in École Lawrence in Bapaume, along with the Swift and Goodinson table and casket.

The Alderman Wardley Crèche, originally for pre-school children had become an infant school after WW2 and it was probably at this time it was renamed 'École Lawrence'.

It was promised that the memorial chairs from the crèche would be replaced. Fortunately the inscription plates were all removed before the Germans took over the place.

Elsie Lawrence was with this Sheffield civic party and received a great reception in Bapaume. She promised to virtually double the size of the crèche and to add a stained glass window in memory of her husband. It was stated that work on the £1,000 crèche extension "will start next week".

Unfortunately, soon after returning to England, Elsie was taken ill and she died at 'Belmont' in Hathersage on 11th December 1946.

It is thought that the extension to the crèche was completed, but that Bapaume never asked for the promised £1,000 (£30,000).

Elsie's funeral also took place at Hathersage Methodist Church, on Monday 16th December 1946. A guard of honour formed up outside, from some seventy of her employees attending, many of them women. Four departmental foremen were bearers. Her estate was valued at £34,957 - 9 - 7d, gross, £29,646 - 4 - 9d net. About £900,000 in 2011 terms.

Under the terms of her will, made on 16th April 1946 just before she went to France, she left legacies to her husband, Percy Bradley Lawrence; to her brother, Albert Bolton; and to her nephews and nieces: Arthur Collin Pratt, Cyril Edward Bolton, Winifred Florence Alderson, Robin Collin Howarth, Gladys Loxley, Annie Shipman, Ernest Hunter, Rene Styring, Doris Axelby, Dora Mary Stacey, Arthur Bolton, Elyn Sykes, Mary Bolton, Leslie Bolton, Ronald Hessey; also to her late husband's sister, Beatrice Esther Meace, and to her sister, Emma Whitham.

She also left sums to the Hathersage Methodist Church, the R.N.L.I., the Sheffield Institute for the Blind, the St Dunstan's Institute for Blind Soldiers, the Sheffield Cripple Aid Association, the Imperial Fund for Cancer Research, and the National Society for the Prevention of Cruelty to Animals.

The majority of her possessions however, she left in trust with instructions for them to be used "in establishing objects of charity and benevolence".

John Richmond, trustee of the 'Elsie Lawrence Trust' that was established, notes that since her death many Hathersage organisations (as well as many others outside the village) have at various times benefited from the Trust's donations. These include the Memorial Hall, the Moorlands Retirement Home, the Horticultural Society, the Bowling Club, the Scouts, the Guides, the First Responders, the Football Club, the Cricket Club, the Swimming Pool (King George's Field), the Village Choir and the Methodist Church.

After Elsie's death, 'Belmont', the Lawrence's house in Hathersage, was sold on 7th June 1947 to Mr C O Birtles, for £3,500 (£105,000 today with inflation, although its current market price will be about five times this figure). The field opposite on Jaggers Lane, which belonged to the house, was sold to Mr Littlewood for £75, on part of which the present Holly House was built with stone from Outseats Parish quarry.

When Mr Birtles, the new owner, later sold 'Belmont', he kept the bowling green and the field above it and these later became part of the property that his son and wife acquired: 'Beeches Barn' on Ranmoor Hill.

Elsie also had 750 shares in 'Laurel Garages (Hathersage) Ltd'. These were also sold in 1947 for £491-1-8d (£14,730). This was probably the small repair unit, run by Randolph Churchill Taylor and operating out of a part of the Ordnance Arms Hotel barn buildings. Why Mrs Lawrence invested in such a business around 1945, or why it should need so much capital is unclear, unless perhaps it had a second-hand car-selling activity coupled to it.

☞ In the years since their passing...

THE FOLLOWING IS A SNAPSHOT of what has happened in the sixty-five years since Elsie died and the seventy-one since George was killed. It is intended only to bring up-to-date the position and give other snippets of information regarding the various ongoing ventures in which they were involved.

In 1947 the Swimming Club trophies were re-valued for insurance purposes. The Lawrence Championship Cup was valued at £45 (£1,350 today).

Des Williams worked as an attendant at Hathersage swimming pool in 1949, together

with Stuart Burkimsher. To clean the pool they would pull a large weighted brush along the bottom.

All the schools in the Hope Valley would come to use the pool at that time. A junior season ticket then cost 2/6d (£3.50 today).

At about the same time boys had impromptu challenges, jumping off the top diving board onto the second board and then into the water, vying with each other to see who could get closest to the poolside. George Millward apparently won, but he got so close to the side that he split his leg open on the edge of the pool.

In 1954 the 'Winhill Girls', a local Hathersage men's group, who did a lot of charity work and raised funds for various causes, put in a replacement concrete floor after the wooden one in the bandstand had rotted. Around this time the finances generally, of the King George's Field were in a very shaky state. In 1950 the season ticket prices had been increased to 7/6d per child (£9.50) and £1 per adult (£25).

It was probably around this time, the mid 1950's, that the children's paddling pool and sandpit, had to be closed because of vandalism and broken glass being deposited in them, and the acute lack of money to maintain them.

The Hathersage Bowling Green opened a new extension to their pavilion in 2006, and two heraldic emblems commemorating the King George's Field, were obtained from the National Playing Fields Association (since renamed 'Fields in Trust'). These were then erected in prominent places in the Hathersage children's playing field area.

The Hathersage Men's Institute, which had been using the Stanage Hall in 1936, when the Lawrence Hall was built, closed down on 10th July 1939. It was replaced by a new mixed Victory Social Club for those of 14 and over, which was opened by Colonel (Col) R L Craig on Saturday 5th October 1946.

Col R L Craig was also involved when the Hope Valley Football League championship final was played in Hathersage in May 1947, and he presented the 'Lawrence Cup' to the winning captain of Peak Dale Football Club.

On 19th July in 1952, Hope Valley Schools Sports were held on the Hope Sport's Club Ground and a Hathersage pupil, Brenda Gosney, won the Lawrence Cup for Girls. There was also a similar Cup for the boys, both having been donated during GHL's lifetime. It was also noted that on 25th May 1955, that the Hope Valley School Sports Association, held at G & T Earle Ltd, Hope, still included a competition for 'The Lawrence Cup'. Unfortunately there is no longer any trace of either the boys' or girls' cups.

George Lawrence Championship Cup being presented in Hathersage to the captain of Peak Dale FC, by Col R L Craig, 1947

The new Methodist Church acquired a Sunday schoolroom in 1947. This was a wooden building and was positioned behind the Church. Measuring 36yds x 16yds and without a floor, lighting or heating, it was bought for £250 (£7,500). It has been suggested that this is the same hut in which Eric Ollerenshaw later kept his hens at Brontë Cottage on Birley Lane.

Five years later, in 1952 the wooden structure was replaced by a more permanent building, which Messrs Wildgoose built at a cost of £5,785. This work was funded, perhaps partly through Elsie Lawrence's recent legacy, but largely with the money raised from the sale of the Castleton Road Institute, which Marsh Bros had bought for £3,500 in 1945.

In 1969 there had been a suggestion to cover over Longley Park swimming pool but it was decided not to go ahead. There must have been problems in 1975, for repairs had to be made before it was open to the public in June that year. The problems continued however and it was closed again in 1979 because of subsidence, and more temporary repairs had to be made. A scheme was drawn up to replace it with a completely new pool, at a cost of £140,000 (£435,000) but this did not get approval either.

Each year temporary repairs were carried out but the pool remained in a poor state, as in 1982 and 1983, it was decided not to make any charge for admission. Probably around 1989 it was eventually closed completely, because of cracks and vandalism.

Longley Park Pool - abandoned!

Meanwhile Sheffield's other outdoor pool, Millhouses, was attracting private investment. It was suggested that this emphasised the difference in affluence of resources in the south compared with the north of the City.

In France, the Bapaume Maternity School was transferred into the 'École Lawrence' on 7th July 1957.

There exists a letter written in 1971 from Gladys Joan Bell, who had just visited Bapaume, and which was sent to express her thanks for Monsieur le Maire's hospitality. Gladys was the daughter of Maurice Swift who had produced the museum casket and table back in 1939.

Bapaume came to Sheffield's attention again on 25th July 1981, in a 'Star' newspaper article about a proposed Bapaume museum. Bill Hutchinson was requesting, on behalf of the Imperial War Museum, any information from Sheffield, which could be included within it. He later sent a letter on to the newspaper, in which he criticised Sheffield Council for snubbing Bapaume, by refusing to send a representative to hand over the information he had collected. The Leader of Sheffield council at the time, David Blunkett, was quoted as saying the council were clamping down on "courtesy" visits abroad.

Today this museum, which is run by the Archaeological & Historical Society of Bapaume, occupies all of the upstairs rooms of École Lawrence. It is run by volunteers and contains many references to the Lawrences and to Sheffield's association with the town, including a photograph of GHL. Beneath it is displayed the Sheffield coat of arms. On another wall is a picture of Mrs Lawrence distributing the cutlery sets to children in 1939. The downstairs rooms of the building are now used by community groups and for adult education.

Bapaume produced a booklet for the millennium: 'BAPAUME de la BELLE EPOQUE à L'AN 2000', relating its history of the previous 100 years. In it there are many references to the Lawrences and to Sheffield.

Bapaume's population had risen to 4991 by the end of the century.

Sheffield made some attempt to revive its links with Bapaume and Serre after Sheffield Councillor, Jackie Drayton (formerly Jackie Field), had visited Bapaume in August 2001. She met M. Eugène Doria, who had become the local historian. In their museum he showed her the set of engraved knife, fork and spoon, complete with presentation box that was given by the Lawrences to every school child in Bapaume the day the crèche opened in 1939. This particular set was the actual one given to M. Doria, himself then a schoolboy living in Bapaume.

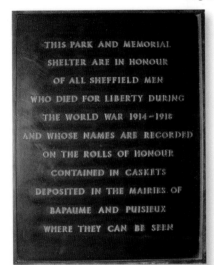

The museum can be visited by appointment, by contacting M. Doria or Baupaume Tourist Information Office at the addresses given in the bibliography at the end of this book.

The Sheffield-Serre Memorial Park & Shelter had fallen into disrepair during and after the Second World War. After the 1946 pilgrimage to the area, a Sheffield Council minute on 17th September 1946 noted a resolution to restore the shelter and provide reforestation over a greater part of the area at an estimated cost of £550, but the shelter was found to be beyond repair and so a new one was built.

Then sixty years later, on 1st July 2006, on the 90th anniversary of the Battle of the Somme, there was a further pilgrimage to the area from the City of Sheffield, organised by Colonel Geoffrey Norton (Y&L) and headed by the Lord Lieutenant of South Yorkshire, Mr David Moody. The Bishop of Sheffield rededicated the newly renovated monument at Serre to the Sheffield City Battalion, in the presence of the Lord Mayor of Sheffield, Cllr Jackie Drayton, along with the Mayors of Rotherham and Barnsley. New signage was put in place at both memorials to help future visitors.

The pilgrims then travelled to nearby Bapaume to attend a reception in the Town Hall and to see École Lawrence and the twelve Sheffield Houses.

Bapaume produced a special informative booklet for the occasion, and it was evident on that visit that Bapaume had not forgotten the material and financial aids, and the dynamics of both courage and help that their English 'godmother' Sheffield had given to them.

Today many visitors to Ypres (Ieper) still call in to the St. George's Church, either to look at the special memorials or to spend a few moments of quiet reflection. Regular services are still held at the Church by the Chaplain, and there is a choir and volunteer committee members, who dedicate their time to help with the running of this special place.

The front door of St. George's Memorial Church is on No. 1, Elverdingsestraat. Services are ecumenical and all are welcome to attend.

Percy Bradley Lawrence became President of Sheffield & Hallamshire County Football Association from 1955 until 1976. He was about 72 when he became President, having joined the Association in 1921. There was a picture of him published in the 1936 '50 years' Jubilee banquet booklet when he was a Vice President.

He died in 1976 and the Methodist Church again benefited from the Lawrences, for he also left them a legacy of £1,000 (£5,000).

Percy Bradley Lawrence was still a director of George H Lawrence Ltd in 1947 when the company received a government war reparations grant, to rebuild the Nursery Street works. As the original offices had remained largely undamaged, and they continued to use these during the war, this grant only covered about 75% of the property. This resulted in inconvenient stairs linking the old office and the new works because of the difference in floor levels. The surviving office section of the old works was in fact part of the original Children's Hospital and it now received just a rendering applied to the external face of the old brickwork. The premises retained the old 'Laurel Works' name and by December 1948 it was back in full production.

By 1957 the Laurel Razor Blade Company (George H Lawrence Ltd) was being run by Percy Bradley Lawrence (PBL) and his son, but making mainly surgical and industrial blades. The razor blade work had virtually gone with the advent of stainless steel blades.

Stainless steel razor blades had long been a vision of the industry, but Wilkinson Sword was the first to successfully develop the process and they patented it.

Even so, some time afterwards, two Wilkinson Sword employees left them and formed the 'Jewel Blade Company'. They started manufacturing stainless steel blades themselves at their Penistone Road, Sheffield works, which Wilkinson Sword tried unsuccessfully to prevent.

'Jewel' was later to become a subsidiary of Swann Morton Ltd.

Most of the Lawrence Company's work was then supplying modelling blades to Humbrol Paints, manufacturers of balsa wood models, to include in their kits.

Humbrol eventually bought this side of the business so they could have the production 'in-house' in their Hull factory and they took the equipment and some key 'Laurel' employees over there with them.

The George H Lawrence Ltd company and the Nursery Street premises were eventually bought by the Grunwerg family business in about 1964.

Many of GHL's old workforce maintained that long after he had been killed, they continued to experience George's presence in the Nursery Street premises, and every time a curtain blew or a door closed on its own, it would be put down to George. After the Grunwerg takeover, Charles Grunwerg (a self-professed sceptic of such events) told how he experienced this phenomenon for himself. It was one Sunday when working alone there in Nursery Street, that he felt the temperature drop, heard a noise, turned round and there was GHL - or rather his ghost - which then evaporated away!

...there was GHL - or rather his ghost which then evaporated away!

Since its development in about 1928, the Lawrences 'Ladies' razor had proved a lasting success, but its production became difficult after the nationalisation of the steel industry. Orders for under a ton of the necessary steel strip was considered uneconomical and GHL Ltd had to obtain stocks from Sweden. This eventually proved unsustainable and together with a failure to keep up investment in new equipment, made the end of the company inevitable. It ceased trading in about 1973.

In each of their wills, both Elsie and Percy Bradley had remembered William Allen, the company secretary at George H Lawrence Ltd, in recognition of his loyalty and long service to the company.

I Grunwerg Ltd moved out of the Nursery Street premises around 1985, and put the premises up for sale. Their nameplates, together with those of G H Lawrence Ltd, W Nodder & Co Ltd, and A J Boswell, clearly remained on the entrance door.

Although not trading, George H Lawrence Ltd was not finally dissolved until 20th August 1991, and the works were eventually demolished in December 2008.

Rebuilt bomb damaged works
until finally demolished in 2008

Myths

MY RESEARCH HAS UNCOVERED instances of where there have been suggestions of George Lawrence's involvement, which has not been borne out by the facts. In an effort to prevent such ideas becoming established as the truth, I will attempt to set the record straight.

For instance, during the 1920's and 1930's there were several outdoor swimming pools developed in Sheffield. One was Bowden Housteads Wood Bathing Pool. Built during 1926 to provide work for the unemployed, mainly out-of-work miners. Sheffield Parks and Burial Grounds Committee Minutes of 21st July 1925 give details of the sanction to borrow £1200 for the pool. Significantly Ald Wardley was the chairman of this committee, with whom George later became very much involved, but the date is well before GHL started his benevolent gestures and there was no mention of GHL's involvement with Bowden Housteads pool.

It was interesting to read that in those days mixed bathing was not encouraged and this pool was open for ladies only on Wednesdays, and on Sundays from 6 am to 12 noon.

The pool was probably closed down by 1939 or soon after.

The Millhouses Park Pool was opened on Thursday 15th August 1929 by the Lord Mayor of Sheffield, but there is no mention or evidence of Lawrence's suggested involvement. Again this development was undertaken before GHL really started funding such projects.

On the other hand, a letter from Irene M Lloyd to the press on 5th July 1981 indicated that GHL had offered to improve the Rivelin Valley swimming pool in the 1930's. She said the Sheffield City Council had rejected this offer and the pool subsequently became derelict.

At various times when reproducing photographs of the opening of the crèche, Bapaume has incorrectly identified Mr Lawrence as the 'Lord Mayor' of Sheffield.

An aerial view of Hathersage in 1938
highlighting features of the village which were to
benefit from the involvement of George Lawrence

1 Sandpit and paddling pool
2 Bowling Green
3 Swimming Pool
4 Tennis Courts
5 Lawrence Hall
6 The old Methodist Wesleyan Chapel
7 Site of the new Methodist Church

 **Facts**

JUST HOW MUCH MONEY DID GHL GIVE AWAY? This is impossible to determine accurately, but we do know that money he donated to major enterprises in Hathersage alone was (in 2011 terms, based on RPI increases): School: £1,000, Bowling Green: £100,000, Swimming Pool: £350,000, Pool Heating: £10,000, Lawrence Hall: £25,000, Methodist Church: £330,000, Organ: £38,000, Ambulance and Fire Pump £40,000 and various sports' cups: £2,000. A total of at least £896,000 that we know of.

If one was to undertake these same projects at today's estimated costs, the total would be more than £1,000,000.

His intentions were always to benefit the community's physical and spiritual well-being, without any strings or recognition.

We have been able to determine the character of the man through his various actions, but do we know what prompted him to be so generous?

In his speech at the opening of the Hathersage Swimming Pool he suggested that: *"those present, when they got home, should take down their Bible and read the 'Parable of the Talents', and there they would find the true motive behind my efforts"*. (Matthew 25 vv 14-26.)

At the opening of the Methodist Church on 30th December 1939 he said that as a boy, more than 40 years previously, in the Surrey Street Methodist Church in Sheffield, he received a book prize on Missionary Sunday. He recalled that on the collecting boxes were the words "It is better to give than to receive" which at the time seemed all wrong to him, yet these prizes for collecting for the missions were still in his home.

He also said: "I have found that throughout life I have been blessed, and I will endeavour to share those blessings with others. I also realize that the more blessings I give to my fellow men, the more blessings I receive".

And again: "I wanted to use my money in my own lifetime, to do good to the greatest number of people".

Very Christian ideals indeed.

"I wanted to use my money in my own lifetime to do good to the greatest number of people".

In an interview with GHL's engineer, Ted Flint said they were producing a million blades a week by 1939 at a gross profit of 5/3d a gross. This would mean they were making about £1,800 (£90,000) gross profit a week before any overhead costs. In what must have been a fiercely competitive market, this figure would seem excessive, and it is unlikely that Ted would know the exact figures. However one can see how GHL could afford to pay for all his philanthropic ventures. The overriding fact remains that he did willingly distribute a very large proportion of his wealth.

Nor was it only his money he was generous with. Even though he had a company that demanded considerable attention, and was a director of Sheffield United Football Club, and was also a Rural District and Parish councillor, he still gave freely of his time to many phil-anthropic ventures. He was evidently a strong character and personality and pushed his projects through with immense drive and enthusiasm.

When he had made his mind up to do something, nothing got in his way, and he did not just leave things to others or to chance.

The timescale for completion of several of the ventures was mind-boggling, illustrating his intense attention to detail.

He must have applied the same dedication to his business affairs. He not only expanded his factory and installed the most modern production equipment; he had to be a very energetic, dedicated and persuasive salesman. This would involve him in a great deal of travel, in order to produce the necessary orders to take up the factory's output. All of which suggests to us why he was so successful.

"I made my money in Sheffield and Sheffield shall have the benefit of it."

Memorials

SO WE REALISE HOW, since his arrival in the village, Hathersage benefited hugely from his largesse. We can appreciate that the recent success of the village, in winning the 'Central England' round of the '2009 England Calor Village of the Year' competition, thus reaching the last five finalists in the country, owes more than a little to this man.

2011 marks the 75th anniversary of the opening of his Hathersage Swimming Pool, providing a timely reminder of the immense benefits received by so many from the Lawrences. A legacy which all Hathersage inhabitants surely have a duty to maintain for those following on behind, and which presents an opportunity to honour and remember a very special person.

Certainly the Parish Councils of Hathersage and Outseats have carried on their responsibility to the pool in this respect. Just this year, (2011) they have carried out a major repair of the pool basin and replacement of the covers at a cost of approximately £80,000.

To meet the public's increased expectation of safety, regulations have multiplied, while ever-increasing financial burdens have called for more ingenious answers, helped by some noteworthy donations, which have occasionally been forthcoming from individuals. Often on an anonymous basis.

The voluntary Hathersage Playing Field Committee have done wonders over the years in raising funds to maintain and replace playground equipment.

John Arthur Stead said at George Lawrence's funeral *"Mr Lawrence did not need a tombstone. His memorials were to be seen on every hand. Generations yet unborn will rise to bless his name and thank him for his generous gifts".*

This plaque is to thank
George H. Lawrence
(1888 - 1940)
for his benevolence in donating
the land and money for developing
this open air swimming pool,
opened in 1936, for the parishioners
of Hathersage and Outseats.

Commemorative plaque fixed to the bandstand by Hathersage Swimming Club in 2010

In another time he might have received some accolade, maybe even a knighthood? But probably because he died early in the war, and was careful not to have his name associated with his many gifts, he has, to a large extent, been forgotten.

In more recent years, efforts have been made in Hathersage to keep his name alive.

Since 2009 a photographic recognition of him, has been on display in the Lawrence Hall and in 2010 a plaque was fixed within Hathersage Swimming Pool commemorating that gift from him.

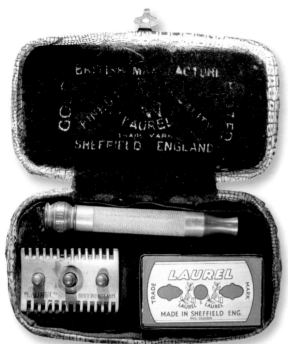

Gold plated 'Laurel' razor in
Kelham Island Museum, Sheffield

While Hathersage has few dedicated mementos of his favours, there are none that are obvious in Sheffield. Cllr Jackie Drayton was quoted as saying that Sheffield had its 'Firth' Park and its 'Mappin' and 'Graves' Galleries, but no mention of Lawrence.

In Sheffield the only remaining memento of him seems to be a boxed, gold plated 'Laurel' razor in Kelham Island museum, which at one time bore the label "originally owned by George Lawrence the Razor King". Unfortunately this was damaged in the 2008 River Don flooding of the premises and the label was not replaced. There is also the framed copy of the letter from Stan Laurel in 1932, which George H Lawrence Ltd had used in their advertising, and now hangs in the entrance to I Grunwerg Ltd's premises in Rockingham Street.

He is generally well-remembered in Bapaume, France, for there is the École Lawrence and a museum where he is commemorated.

In 2003, Cllr Jackie Drayton did her best to rekindle Sheffield's links with Bapaume, when she organised an exhibition in the Sheffield Town Hall, commemorating GHL and his connections with the French town, and there are still regular pilgrimages to the Sheffield WW1 memorials in the area. Yet today that town receives very few visitors from Sheffield, although they see many who come all the way from Australia.

École Lawrence, Baupaume, 2009

Who will take on the task of persuading Sheffield City Council to commemorate George Lawrence, and also once more have the City officially recognise their French 'goddaughter' Bapaume?

"Mr Lawrence did not need a tombstone. His memorials were to be seen on every hand"

☞ ACKNOWLEDGEMENTS

I acknowledge with grateful thanks those who have allowed me to use their photographs, facts or memories, or help in any other way, including (but probably not exclusively): Jackie Drayton, Lord Mayor of Sheffield 2006-2007; George Lawrence's family - Katy Burgin, Christopher Holmes, Mike Garrett and Geoff Meace; also Heather Rodgers and Barbara Wilson for their scrapbooks; Eileen Smith, Chris Eyre, Sheffield & Hallamshire County Football Association; Bryan Bond, Hope Valley Amateur Football League; Alison Duce, Kelham Island Museum; Tom Ward, Wardonia Company; Eugène Doria of Bapaume Museum; Andrew Poole and Catherine Nicklin of Hathersage Church of England School; Stuart 0742 at Sheffield History.co.uk; and Croft House Settlement, Photofinishers Ltd, English Heritage Buildings at Risk Register, Grace Pritt, George Elliott, Peter Miles, Rachel Hudson, Albert Cooper, Roger Dickson, Bob Stamper, Paul Wilson, Keith Gosling, Dot Birtles, Eric Sharman, Diane Cone, Vera Bennett, Winnie Roadknight, Ralph Gulliver, Rennie Bell, Ray Platts, Peter Taylor, Hazel & Andy Jamieson, Peter Jones, John Hardwick, Alfred Prince, Gordon Haines, Barbara Bradwell, Dorothy Harrison, and Joan McKenna. My profound apologies to others I may have missed.

Thanks are also due to Hathersage village organisations: the Bowling Club, the Swimming Club, the Methodist Church, the Village Centre Group, the Football Club, the Memorial Hall, and the Historical Society.

In addition I am indebted to,

John Richmond, trustee of the Elsie Lawrence Trust;

Geoffrey Norton, Vice President of the York & Lancaster Regiment;

Jennifer Fox, Peak District Methodist Circuit Archivist;

Chris Hobbs, for his website on my subject. See the link below;

The Ken Hawley Collection Trust, c/o Kelham Island Museum, Alma Street, Sheffield, S3 8RY, for the transcript of an interview with Ted Flint. (ref SHEKH:avct0033). See their website link below;

Charles Grunwerg of I Grunwerg Ltd;

The Municipality of Ghent City Archives, Abrahamstraat 13, 9000 Ghent, Belgium;

The Bapaume Tourist Information Office, 31 Place Faidherbe, 62450 Bapaume, France, tel 03 21 59 89 84;

The Bapaume Archaeological & Historical Society (SOCIÉTÉ ARCHÉOLOIQUE ET HISTORIQUE DE BAPAUME ET SA RÉGION): Monsieur Eugène Doria, 54 Faubourg de Péronne, 62450 BAPAUME, France;

The Sheffield Local Studies Library and Sheffield Archives, for photographs and archives research;

The Derbyshire Local Studies Library and Records Office, for archives research;

Companies House records.

BIBLIOGRAPHY

Sheffield City Council Minutes: 2nd November 1938; 17th September 1946.

Sheffield Parks & Burials Committee Minutes: 21st July 1925; 13th June 1926.

Sheffield Telegraph and Sheffield Telegraph & Independent newspaper articles including those of: 7th July 1920; 14th July 1920; 27th July 1920; 17th August 1920; 5th August 1922; 11th Aug 1929; December 1930 (industrial supplement); 26th May 1931; 5th Aug 1932; 22nd May 1933; 3rd June 1935; 20th April 1936; 27th June 1936; 27th July 1936; 6th November 1937; 16th February 1938; 11th July 1938; July 1939; 5th November 1938; 29th February 1940; 30th May 1940; 16th December 1940; 3rd June 1946; 6th June 1946; 12th December 1946; 2nd November 2001.

Sheffield Star newspaper articles: 21st April 1936; 14th December 1940; 28th May 1946; 25th March 1947; 25th July 1981, 8th October 1981.

Sheffield Daily Independent newspaper articles: 1st November 1937; 11th November 1937.

The Peak Advertiser article: 20th September 1993.

Derbyshire Times newspaper articles: 12th November 1937; 11th March 1938; 5th May 1938; 28th July 1939; 4th August 1939; 29th September 1939; 6th October 1939; 5th January 1940; 31st May 1940; 20th December 1940; 27th December 1940; 3rd January 1941; 26th December 1941.

Daily Express newspaper article: 16th December 1940.

Guardian Newspaper article: 16th July 1936.

Hathersage Church of England School Log Book 31st October 1934.

Hathersage Memorial Hall Management Meetings Minute Books 1935 - 1958.

Hathersage Swimming Club Minute Book and Cash Book 1936.

Hathersage Auxiliary Hospital 1914-1918 by Peter Miles 1993.

Hathersage Parish Council Minutes 13th September 1936; 17th September 1936; 2nd November 1941.

The First Hundred Years 1894 to 1994 Extracts of Hathersage Parish Council Minutes, compiled by Neil Fletcher.

Outseats Parish Council Minutes 24th April 1938.

Hathersage in the Peak by Barbara Buxton, Phillimore 2005.

Hathersage Methodist Church by Rev John R Farley 1989.

Who's Who. (Sheffield United Football Club publications 2009).

The Biography, p 160, p189, (Sheffield United Football Club publications 2006).

The Jimmy Hagan Story, pps 29, 56, by Roger Barnard, Tempus Publishing 2007.

Edith Cavell 1865-1915 - A Norfolk Heroine by Rev Phillip McFadyen and Rev David Chamberlin, 2011.

Sheffield Blitz by Paul License - ('The Roll Of Honour'), p110, Sheffield Newspapers Ltd.

Sheffield at War 1939-194, by Clive Hardy, Archive Publications 1987.

Sheffield's Date with Hitler by Neil Anderson, ACM Retro 2010.

Sheffield in the 1930's by Peter Harvey, p55, Sheaf Publishing.

Sheffield Bapaume Pilgrimage programme, July 1939.

Re-dedication of Sheffield City Battalion Monument, programme, 1st July 2006.

BAPAUME de la BELLE EPOQUE à L'AN 2000',

The Sheffield Telegraph 1855-1925 - Sir W C Leng & Co (Sheffield Telegraph) Ltd.

Kelly Trade Directories Sheffield.

White Trade Directories Sheffield.

1851 Census ref HO 107/2337, folio 211 p 25.

1901 Census, Census ref RG13/4368. p 30, sched 176, 15th March 1901.

Indiscretions of Lady Susan by Lady Susan Townley, chapter XIII, Thornton Butterworth.

For further reading regarding the Battle of the Somme and the Sheffield City Battalion see:

Sheffield City Battalion: the 12th (Service) Battalion York & Lancaster Regiment by Ralph Gibson and Paul Oldfield – Leo Cooper, 1994: ISBN 1-84415 423 8, - Sheffield Local Studies Library 940.43 SF

Sheffield Soldiers Killed in Action 1st July 1916, by Ian C Pearson, - Published by the author, 1991 - Sheffield Local Studies Library 940.467S

It was a Lovely Summer's Day, by J Roe & W Campbell - Extracts from interviews with Reg Glenn and other Sheffield survivors of the Somme. Published by the authors 1987, - Sheffield Local Studies Library 940.3SQ

First day on the Somme, by Martin Middlebrook - Allen Lane 1971, Sheffield Local Studies Library ref 940.4272 - loan copies are available.

World War 1 Roll of Honour of Sheffield Combatants Sheffield Local Studies Library. Ref 940.467S.

Details of the 1.7 million casualties of the First World War are available from the Commonwealth War Graves Commission website: www.cwgc.org

Sheffield-Serre Memorial Park:
www.greatwar.co.uk/somme/memorial-sheffield-park.htm

Chris Hobbs website re G H Lawrence; www.chrishobbs.com/

The Ken Hawley Collection Trust:
www.sheffield.ac.uk/hawley/trust.html

Laurel & Hardy information: www.laurelandhardyforum.com

Edith Cavell: www.edithcavell.org.uk

Hathersage today... some of the legacy of the 'forgotten philanthropist'